Global Development
Environment Se

Series Editors
Richard M. Auty and Robert B. Potter

Economic Development and the Environment

Economic Development and the Environment

A Comparison of Sustainable Development with Conventional Development Economics

Raymond F. Mikesell

MANSELL

First published in 1992 by
Mansell Publishing Limited, *A Cassell Imprint*
Villiers House, 41/47 Strand, London WC2N 5JE, England
387 Park Avenue South, New York, NY 10016-8810, USA

Reprinted 1993

Reprinted in paperback 1995

British Library Cataloguing in Publication Data

Mikesell, Raymond F.
  Economic Development and the Environment:
  Comparison of Sustainable Development
  with Conventional Development Economics.
  – (Global Development & the Environment
  Series)
  I. Title.   II. Series
  338.9009172

  ISBN 0–7201–2138–8 (Hardback)
  ISBN 0–7201–2267–8 (Paperback)

Library of Congress Cataloging-in-Publication Data

Mikesell, Raymond Frech.
   Economic development and the environment: a comparison of
sustainable development with conventional development economics/
Raymond F. Mikesell.
      p.   cm. – (Global development and the environment series)
   Includes bibliographical references and index.
   ISBN 0–7201–2138–8 (Hardback)
   ISBN 0–7201–2267–8 (Paperback)
   1. Economic development – Environmental aspects.   2. Economic
development projects.   I. Title.   II. Series : Global development
and the environment.
HD75.6.M55   1992
363.7—dc20   92-16983
                                                                    CIP

Typeset by Colset Private Limited, Singapore
Printed and bound in Great Britain by
Biddles Limited, Guildford and King's Lynn

Contents

Foreword

The principal aim of the Global Development and the Environment series is to provide an outlet for scholarly work covering important aspects of Third World development and change. The series is aimed at a multidisciplinary audience and it is intended that the issues covered will be treated from a variety of different disciplinary perspectives – economic, social and political, historical and environmental among them. At the same time, we are aware of the need to achieve balance with respect to the various regions of the Third World that are covered by volumes in the series, not least because of the striking heterogeneity that is so characteristic of the nations making up what we refer to in shorthand terms as the 'developing world'. In essence, we are seeking to promote the publication of works that deal in a rigorous manner with Third World themes and issues that are of topical interest and pressing social importance.

One important objective of the series is to encourage new and bold perspectives on development problems and issues. A second key objective is to develop inter-country comparisons that achieve balanced coverage of the principal regions of the world. It is hoped that such inter-country comparisons will shed new light on the ways in which differing social, cultural, economic, political, ecological and natural resource systems condition responses to global processes of change.

The series is thereby built around two closely related themes: globalization and environmental change. Globalization is a major trend affecting contemporary Third World countries. It is reflected in the diffusion of capital and technology, the evolution of new production systems and the spread of Western lifestyles among elites and other groups. It is also witnessed in the increasing importance of multinational corporations. Yet it is clear that the processes of global restructuring and change are affecting various regions and nations at different rates and in a variety of different ways. For example, large income gaps have opened up within countries such as those of Latin America and the Caribbean, while pressures on resources vary markedly among the various rural areas of sub-Saharan Africa. Similarly, rates of economic growth have diverged sharply in East Asia. It is clear that patterns of production are becoming increasingly heterogeneous when viewed at the international level, while patterns of consumption and associated aspirations are frequently converging on what might be described as a global norm. However, such patterns of consumption are likely to be found to be strongly differentiated when examined in different groups and areas at the local scale.

Environmental change is strongly affected by the globalization of development, whether through the clearance and destruction of rainforests, the occurrence of industrial accidents, the despoliation of attractive environments, indigenous cultures and socioeconomic landscapes by the demands of international tourism, or the consequences of global warming for sustainable patterns of development and resource use. The examination of the interacting socio-political and environmental causes of these problems, along with practical responses, stands as a further major theme of the series.

This volume by the distinguished American economist, Ray Mikesell, is a particularly fitting one to help establish the series. It is a pioneering work that addresses the important task of integrating sustainability criteria into development economics. The book reaches the optimistic conclusion that many of the objectives of the two perspectives do in fact converge. Although sustainable development is unlikely to subsume development economics, the latter is sufficiently flexible to incorporate many of the objectives of sustainability.

Professor Mikesell advances his thesis in lucid non-technical prose which accords well with the series' intention of reaching an interdisciplinary audience. Liberal use is made of case studies and empirical examples to illustrate the general points made in the opening chapters of the book. In this way Professor Mikesell has laid a strong foundation for the Mansell series upon which subsequent more specialized studies will build.

Rick Auty   Rob Potter
Lancaster, Lancashire   Englefield Green, Surrey
England   England

1
Introduction

What is called *sustainable development* builds on an economic discipline that has changed in content, methodology, and major objectives over time. Whether sustainable development will be the paradigm for future academic textbooks on economic development is yet unclear, but it is certain to have a major influence on the field.

As every student of economics knows, economic development as an organized discipline began with Adam Smith's *Wealth of Nations* (1776), which was concerned with the long-run course of the British economy. Preoccupation with economic development by British economists continued through the first half of the nineteenth century, after which Victorian optimism led them to the conviction that economic growth in Britain, and perhaps in Western Europe and North America as well, was inevitable. Since most of the rest of the world consisted of colonies that supplied raw materials to the economic centers, little attention was paid to their becoming anything else. Except for the important work of Joseph A. Schumpeter in *The Theory of Economic Development* (1911, 1934), which showed the critical role of the entrepreneur in growth, economic development was largely dormant until the explosion of independent, nationalistic states after the Second World War – states that were anxious to achieve both political and economic independence from their colonial masters. Since then, this discipline has been largely concerned with how non-Western countries can attain self-generating growth (without continuous foreign aid) and broadly based economic and social progress.

The field of economic development has gone through several phases since it became recognized as both an academic discipline and a prescription for government actions and policies in developing countries following the Second World War.[1] Economic development evolved as a loosely integrated combination of other recognized fields, such as production, international trade, investment, monetary and fiscal policy, and agricultural and industrial sector analysis. The emphasis given to each field in the formula for growth has shifted with economic ideology and with what has been shown to succeed in other countries. Early development economists were not satisfied with the traditional explanation of poverty: poor resources, ethnic-based lack of motivation, and non-Western social order. The reasons for the failure of poor countries to grow were found in the imperfections of domestic and world markets; distortions in the prices of labor, capital, and foreign exchange; and a lack of direction and coordination of investment. Many early development economists argued that while growth evolved over centuries in the developed countries without government control and direction, developing countries should bypass this long stagnation period by adopting and executing the proper economic plan. Because rapid industrialization appeared to be the paradigm for growth, state industrial enterprise and subsidized private industry should lead the way. Agriculture was usually neglected because it was not regarded as an engine of growth. In countries where governments paid particular attention to agriculture, it often took the form of land reform designed for wealth distribution, and the creation of government-controlled cooperatives or state-operated farms designed for the capture of resource rents by the government. Except possibly for plantation production for export, little attention was paid to increasing agricultural productivity. Yet raising the real incomes of the bulk of the populations of poor countries depends heavily upon raising the productivity of the rural sectors.

The early development models made growth a function of capital inputs, with particular emphasis on foreign capital. In the broadly accepted two-gap growth model, one gap was that between the level of investment required to achieve a target rate of growth and the level of domestic saving, while the other gap was between import requirements to maintain the required investment and export earnings. Both gaps might need to be filled by external capital, but the dominant constraint on growth was foreign exchange (Chenery, 1966). Planning and government intervention, including direct government investment, were believed necessary to channel investment into the proper sectors. Sustained growth required that growth be balanced in the sense that one sector should not get too far out of line with others, since growth depended upon sector complementarity and mutual support. Thus, infrastructure should not proceed more rapidly than industry or agriculture, raw materials production should not outrun manufacturing, and consumer goods output should not outrun the capital goods industries. Governments gave considerable attention to the pattern and timing of investment in various sectors in the preparation of multi-year development plans and their implementation.

By the early 1970s, both the macroeconomic two-gap models and multi-year development planning had fallen into disfavor. Foreign aid programs designed to fill the hypothetical gap between imports required for target growth rates and foreign exchange earnings did not produce the growth targets and the five-year development plans were almost never realized. Moreover, the World Bank (which replaced the US Agency for International Development (USAID) as the principal source of external development assistance) was never guided by aggregate growth models and became disillusioned with the comprehensive development plans. Instead, the World Bank emphasized sectoral planning and detailed project formulation. During the 1970s, development economists formulated more complex models for growth, made growth less capital oriented, placed less emphasis on 'balanced' growth in terms of coordinated sectoral expansion, and gave greater emphasis to the flexible response of investment allocation to market forces. They also began to advocate competitive markets, increased export incentives, and the promotion of savings and domestic and foreign investment. Broadly based development, including social services such as education and health and the elimination of poverty, replaced maximizing the growth rate as the major development objective. Finally, development economics began to recognize agricultural productivity for the peasant farmers as an essential requirement for development.

In the 1980s development economics became largely policy oriented, emphasizing free markets for goods, capital and foreign exchange, and the privatization of state enterprises. The remarkable success of the Asian developing countries (Korea, Singapore, Hong Kong, and Thailand) that liberalized their internal markets and foreign trade provided the paradigm for development progress everywhere. Government policy failure rather than market failure was seen as the principal cause of low or negative growth, and developing countries were counseled to look inward for their economic salvation, not to international commodity stabilization schemes or increased aid from the industrial countries. The large flow of external capital during the 1970s and early 1980s, which led to the debt crisis, came to be seen not as a promoter of growth but as a curse, because government management failed to channel the capital into productive uses. Inflation, not internal market failure, was regarded as the major source of price distortions that misdirected resources. A primary objective of government was price stability achieved by balanced budgets and monetary restraint, rather than by intervention in the market process. Another important objective of government was investment in human capital in the form of education, health, sanitation, and farmer and worker training. These objectives were promoted by the international development banks and bilateral aid agencies. The

World Bank and the International Monetary Fund (IMF) began making structural adjustment loans (SALs) designed to assist governments in changing their policies without inflicting hardships on their economies – especially on the poorest segment. The SALs were reasonably successful in some countries, but in others, such as Brazil, they failed miserably.

The revolution of the 1980s did not mean that development economists had become libertarians or that they adopted all the criticisms of state intervention preached by Peter T. Bauer (1972). Not only is enthusiasm for privatization and market liberalization not universal, but there is considerable dissension about the regulatory role of government in both developing and industrial economies. Development management is a political as well as economic process, and development economists reflect a wide spectrum of political ideologies. In the USA this divergence is seen in the current debate among leading economists on how this country should combat the loss of world markets and technological leadership to Japan. Here, as in development economics, the economists' view of the role of government is crucial. Albert Fishlow (1991, p. 1736), in his incisive review of development economic literature, states: 'What development economics lacks is an adequate theory of government policy. . . . Political economy models do not yet combine underlying economic behavior, the distribution of political power and the attributes of the technocracy in a way that makes them empirically powerful.' There is a growing reluctance to rely on government intervention because in the past it has suffocated the dynamic forces that promote growth and created disparities that misdirect resources. But this does not necessarily mean that government regulation cannot improve social welfare without impeding economic progress.

The issue of the regulating role of government in development management has arisen through the introduction of the environment into development theory and policy. The integration of the environment into development economics dates at least from the 1960s, but environmental economics still does not play a major role in the leading economic development textbooks or other well-known treatises on the subject. In the late 1980s and early 1990s a few books featuring 'sustainable development' in their titles were published, but at the time of writing, no book has appeared combining the major themes and analytical approaches of sustainable development with the full range of topics dealt with in standard development textbooks.[2] This is somewhat surprising given the large amount of literature, including textbooks, on the economics of the environment and natural resources. However, given the attention being paid to the subject by the multilateral development banks (MDBs), the United Nations (UN) agencies, the Organisation for Economic Co-operation and Development (OECD), the bilateral development assistance agencies, and influential nongovernmental institutions (NGOs) in both developed and developing countries, sustainable development must be regarded as an important revolution in development objectives and policies.

Environmental protection and resource management for sustainable development requires government regulation, which to some degree conflicts with the modern trend in development economics in the 1980s toward market freedom and deregulation. Most environmental economists believe in competitive markets and favor economic incentives over 'command and control' instruments for achieving environmental and resource conservation goals. Nevertheless, requiring producers to internalize the social costs of their pollution, or preventing private owners of natural resources from depleting or degrading resources required by future generations, necessarily entails some government intervention in markets or interference with private property rights. Environmental problems also arise in foreign trade and investment. Hence, policy conflicts may occur between exponents of free trade and capital movements on the one hand, and advocates of sustainable development on the other. Long-range environmental intervention may involve decisions on the location of manufacturing or processing facilities, the development and use of alternative energy resources, and the choice of agricultural technology – decisions normally made by market forces in a private enterprise economy. Opinion on how far government should go in planning and managing the economy (or to what extent government should be trusted) differs greatly among environmentalists.

Is sustainable development economics a reversal of the trend of conventional economic development toward economic liberalism, deregulation, and privatization? To a considerable degree, sustainable development expands the role of government in regulation and in directly controlling the use of natural resources. However, the objectives of control differ from those in the past. Government intervention is not designed to promote economic growth, but rather to prevent economic activity from overwhelming the pollution absorptive capacity of the environment, or depleting or degrading the natural resource base. For some environmental economists, sustainable development has far-reaching social equity goals on both a national and global basis. Environmental economists differ on the degree to which government should be responsible for a range of social welfare services and ecological concerns.

Preoccupation with social and ecological issues, such as the preservation of species, is closely associated with sustainable development, but this is not what distinguishes it from conventional economics, because many conventional economists have these same concerns. Nor is the unique character of sustainable development to be found in its emphasis on pollution abatement and internalizing adverse environmental impacts. After all, external diseconomies and the 'polluter pays' principle have been in economic literature for at least 75 years. The distinguishing characteristic of sustainable development is the maintenance of the natural resource base, including the waste absorptive capacity of the environment, for the use of future generations so that their opportunities to maintain or advance their well being are undiminished. This objective has led to the use of resource accounting, and the development of techniques to avoid discounting future benefits and costs in choosing among alternative allocations of natural resources.

In the following chapters the unique features of sustainable development are examined in detail, along with the ways in which the introduction of sustainable development principles alters the content and analysis of conventional development. Chapter 2 examines the conceptual content and some theoretical issues encountered in sustainable development. It is shown that while most of the analytical techniques employed are the same as those found in conventional development theory, the intergenerational concern for preserving the natural resource base broadens and complicates the social welfare function. Resource accounting is used instead of conventional national product accounting, and social costs include global externalities, even within the frame of reference of national welfare.

Chapter 3 reviews the environmental and resource problems created by development projects and programs. The internalization of the external impacts of development activities could be readily embodied in conventional development policy and practice, and failure to do so is a basic criticism levied by environmentalists that many conventional development economists are now beginning to recognize. In other words, there is no doctrinal dispute involved. Projects and programs need to be evaluated in terms of their full social costs, but many of these costs have been neglected in conventional economics. Chapter 3 also examines the environmental and resource impacts of development on a sectoral basis, and this analysis is complemented by case studies presented in Chapter 6.

Chapter 4 considers how the treatment of major categories of development policies needs to be altered to achieve conformity with sustainable development doctrine. In many cases, this alteration is a matter of emphasis rather than fundamental conflict. An important characteristic of sustainable development economics is the awareness of environmental and natural resource impacts. This does not reflect a fundamental difference from conventional development economics regarding the relevance of these impacts for development – they have simply been ignored in the past.

MDBs have a major influence on Third World development through the projects and programs they finance, the conditions they attach to utilization of their loan funds, and their advisory and technical services. Chapter 5 reviews some of the failures of these institutions to observe sustainable development principles in the past, and traces their conversion to applying them in recent years. The case studies presented in Chapter 6 illustrate environmentally flawed development projects, while Chapter 7 presents case studies regarded as sustainable development successes. MDBs and other external development assistance agencies have supported projects in both categories.

NOTES

1   For an excellent review of post-Second World War economic development literature, see Albert Fishlow (1991).
2   Good examples of recent books on sustainable development are those by Pearce *et al.* (1990), Adams (1990), and Turner (1988). Perhaps the closest approximation to a comprehensive sustainable development treatise that could serve as a textbook is an unpublished manuscript by Pearce and Warford (1991).

REFERENCES

Adams, W.N. (1990) *Green Development: Environment and Sustainability in the Third World*: London and New York: Routledge.
Bauer, Peter T. (1972) *Dissent on Development*. Cambridge, MA: Harvard University Press.
Chenery, Hollis B. (1966) Foreign assistance and economic development. *American Economic Review*, 56, 679–733.
Fishlow, Albert (1991) Review of *Handbook of Development Economics. Journal of Economic Literature*, 29(4), 1728–37.
Pearce, David, Barbier, Edward and Markandya, Anil (1990) *Sustainable Development*. London: Elgar.
Pearce, David and Warford, Jeremy (1991) Environment and economic development. Unpublished manuscript. Forthcoming, Oxford University Press for the World Bank.
Schumpeter, Joseph A. (1911, 1934) *The Theory of Economic Development*. Cambridge, MA: Harvard University Press.
Smith, Adam (1776) *An Inquiry into the Nature and Causes of the Wealth of Nations*. London: Strahan and Cadell (New York: Modern Library (1937) and other reprints).
Turner, R. Kerry (ed.) (1988) *Sustainable Environmental Management*. Boulder, CO: Westview Press.

2

The Introduction of Sustainability to Development Theory: Some Conceptual Theoretical Issues

Introduction

Sustainable development might be described as a 'return to nature' following a century or more of predominant concern with industrialization, trade, and urbanization as the symbols of national progress. This chapter analyzes the natural resource orientation of sustainable development and its application to the measurement and promotion of development. Resource accounting is a key element in this conceptual framework since it treats the natural resource base, including the life support system of the planet, as capital assets whose quantity and productivity must be preserved as a fundamental condition for human progress. This chapter also analyzes the concept of natural resource sustainability and shows how it may either conflict or be in harmony with economic growth. Finally, this chapter describes how projects and programs can be designed and evaluated in accordance with the sustainability criteria presented and compares this process with that found in conventional development economics.

It has become commonplace to say that environmental protection and natural resource conservation are important in any program of economic development. The World Bank and the regional development banks (Asian Development Bank (ADB) and Inter-American Development Bank (IADB)) have been making such statements for the past decade and the term sustainable development has become part of the litany of every agency concerned with promoting Third World development. Yet the mutuality of development and the environment tends to mask the conceptual and theoretical problems encountered in formulating a theory of sustainable development.

These problems arise in part from the imprecise nature of sustainability as a goal and the consequent difficulties in measuring elements of sustainability in ways that indicate progress in achieving it. Conceptual and theoretical problems also abound when environmental and resource factors are introduced into the conventional analysis of growth and development. Although sustainable development is revolutionary, it will not replace decades of analysis and empirical research concerned with mobilizing labor, capital, and natural resources to achieve conventional development goals. Sustainability requires additional goals for the economic process, but does not replace the conventional ones.

In the past, economic development has been largely oriented to national development since government policies for promoting development can be fully applied only at the national level, and there are severe limitations on the movement of populations across national boundaries. The difficulty with a national or regional approach to sustainable development is that there are global resources, such as the upper atmosphere, the oceans, and biodiversity, that are common to all nations, and limiting their deterioration depends on cooperative actions among nations. It may also be noted that many social scientists believe that the focus of environmental and resource policies should be global rather than national, especially since future national boundaries may be quite different or might not even exist. However, we cannot abandon national development economics for global economics where few policy instruments exist and agreed goals are difficult to reach and harder to implement. We must deal with the theoretical and policy issues on a national basis, while keeping in mind that all economic activity and the very survival of our species depend upon the preservation of common global resources.

The Natural Resource Base and Economic Activity

What distinguishes environmental from traditional economics is the special attention that is given to the interaction between the natural resource base and economic activity. The natural resource base comprises the land and the subsoil, natural plants and animals, oceans, lakes, and rivers and their aquatic life, and the atmosphere and its meteorology. These environmental assets provide services and resource flows that constitute inputs into the production process, and direct utilities to human and other forms of life. All economic activities, including consumption, create waste: effluents into water bodies, air pollution, and solid wastes. These waste products must either be recycled for reuse in the economic process or absorbed by the environment. Not all waste can be recycled – some must be absorbed. For example, when we burn coal for energy, some of it will end up as gas and slag, which must be absorbed. According to the First Law of

Thermodynamics, we cannot create or destroy energy or matter; the natural resources used yield an equivalent amount of products and waste. There are limits to the capacity of the air, water and land to assimilate waste without impairing their functions in production, in supporting life, and in providing environmental amenities.

Environmental economics integrates the natural resource cycle with the economic process. It examines what we must do to maintain the productivity of the resource base by conserving exhaustible resources, by restoring renewable resources, and by limiting unrecycled waste to what can be assimilated by the environment. The activities for preserving the resource base become a part of the cost structure of the economic system, and costs determine prices, which allocate resource uses. Sustainable development provides the additional objective that the productivity of the resource base should not be maximized simply for the present generation, but for all generations.

We can portray the interaction between the natural resource base and the economic system as a flow of natural resource inputs into the production–consumption process and a return flow of waste products to the natural resource base. The problem for sustained development is to maximize the flow of natural resource inputs on a sustained intergenerational basis, while keeping the flow of waste products at a level below which they can be assimilated without impairing the productivity of the natural resource base. Although the global supply of natural resources cannot be expanded, it is possible to increase their productivity by: (a) increasing the output of goods and services per unit of natural resource input; (b) increasing the flow of natural resources per unit of natural stock (limited by biological growth rates); and (c) increasing the end-use efficiency with which goods produced from natural resources yield services to the final user. It is also possible to increase natural resource inputs per unit of waste that must be assimilated. This is achieved by recycling, by limiting waste discharge, and by changing the composition of the waste products so they are easier to assimilate.

The following are examples of increasing the productivity of natural resources:

1 Technologies that reduce the amount of copper or aluminum used in car radiators, or the amount of materials used in constructing buildings, without losing strength or other desired properties.
2 Technologies that increase the rate of growth of trees or plants without causing environmental harm.
3 Technologies that conserve energy by reducing heat loss in buildings or by making cars more energy efficient.
4 Recycling where the energy and other natural resources required for producing recycled products is less than that required for products from natural materials.
5 Eliminating certain chemicals from the production process to reduce the amount of waste, and altering the method of waste disposal (say, from waterways to underground burial) to increase assimilation capacity.

All of the above measures contribute to sustainability by economizing on resource inputs for a given level of output of goods and services, or expanding the capacity of the natural resource base to assimilate waste created by a given level of output. But these measures do not necessarily preserve the natural resource base for future generations, nor do they guarantee future generations a certain level of per capita output.

Alternative Concepts of Sustainability

There are a number of concepts of sustainability which reflect the values and objectives that adherents regard as important.[1] Ecologists concentrate on the degradation of physical resources that sustain life in all its forms. Their objective is to preserve the global ecosystem for future generations and to minimize its current deterioration. Although most ecologists argue for preservation in terms of the contribution to human welfare, others project a reverence for all life and hold that all species have the right to exist, quite apart from any contribution to human welfare (O'Riordan, 1988, p. 30). This approach is sometimes called 'deep ecology.' Most environmentalists tend to view sustainability in terms of the capacity of the natural resource base to maintain and increase human welfare measured in terms of both marketable and nonmarketable goods and services. Perhaps the best-known definition is that given in the Brundtland Report, which advocated 'development that meets the needs of the present without compromising the ability of future generations to meet their own needs' (World Commission on Environment and Development, 1987, p. 43). The obligation to future generations is usually stated in terms of human welfare rather than the inheritance of physical resources. Since the quantity and composition of physical natural resources must inevitably change from generation to generation, what must be passed on is defined in terms of the social benefits the resources are capable of producing when combined with labor and capital. The standard of welfare for future generations varies from a minimum standard of living necessary to perpetuate the human species to a growing level of per capita income expected to be achieved with the aid of technological progress. For many developing countries with high rates of population growth, not even the low present average per capita output could be maintained, given the world's present distribution of natural resources. Thus, some definitions of sustainable development suggest that not only must the value of the global stock of natural resources be maintained, but the resources must be redistributed to assure a certain level of consumption for all people regardless of population growth. Such definitions appear to move away from global resource conservation to an ethic of distributional equity. It appears to me that if global resource conservation is to remain the basic ingredient and rationale for sustainability, intergenerational responsibility should be based on maintaining the productivity of the natural resource base – not on some concept of intergenerational equity.

Sustainability as an economic concept cannot be defined in physical terms, such as maintaining the stock of all natural resources. Some exhaustible resources are inevitably used up in current production, and any mandate that all renewable resources must be restored would not be in accordance with maximizing real income. For example, in a country that is 90 percent covered by forest, it makes little economic sense to replace every tree. As economies grow and become more industrialized, it is necessary to devote some primary areas to agriculture, factories, and homes. To deal with resources in terms of their contribution to economic growth and development, we must convert physical units of different classes of resources into monetary values. Without valuing resources in monetary terms we would have no way of comparing the contributions of different types of resources; say, mineral reserves, old growth forests, and agricultural lands in different uses of the resource, such as mining or timber production or recreation. The per unit value of a particular resource depends upon its contribution to the production of goods and services that people want. Resources have value not simply for commercial production, but also for the direct utilities they provide to humans. Where there are competing uses for a resource, its use should be determined by which use yields the highest social value.

We also need to estimate the monetary costs of destroying or degrading environmental assets. It might be objected that regardless of monetary cost environmental degradation must be rejected, but preventing degradation involves social costs as well; we must adhere to the principle of comparing social benefits with social costs in making decisions. For example, in the Pacific Northwest of the USA, comparisons are being made between the additional costs of electric power and the social benefits of preventing the extinction of certain salmon species threatened by the operation of hydroelectric power dams.

For purposes of analyzing sustainable development, we may recognize three types of resources:

(1) Global resources, such as the atmosphere, oceans, and biodiversity, which are essential to all life and the degradation of which is irreversible, except over very long periods of time. Although we may in time be able to estimate the economic costs of further accumulations of greenhouse gases or of ozone depletion, for the time being at least these estimates are little more than guesses. This does not mean that economic measures cannot be used for controlling actions that impair the global environment, but we are a long way from being able to relate the marginal cost of reducing carbon dioxide emissions to the marginal social damage caused by an additional unit of greenhouse gases.

(2) Renewable natural resources, which include forests, soil fertility, and

the quality of regional air, rivers, lakes, and wetlands. In many cases, costs of both depletion and renewal can be determined. In most cases, destruction and damage to the quality of the resources may be reversed. However, the line between reversible and irreversible damage for some resources is not always clear, and in some cases, such as old-growth ecosystems and severely eroded land, restoration may require hundreds or even thousands of years. In such cases, damage must be regarded as irreversible within the context of the present and near future generations.

(3) Nonrenewable natural resources consisting of minerals, fossil fuels, and plant and animal species that become extinct or whose numbers are reduced to a few examples in zoos and small wildlife refuges. Social values can be estimated for minerals and some progress has been made in valuing wildlife. Most of the natural areas of the world have been occupied and their amenity services impaired. The best we can do is save the remaining parcels for human enjoyment and for making some contribution to the ecological conditions that sustain life.

Maintaining natural resources to produce a constant output

A simple definition of sustainability is maintaining the natural resource base at a level that will enable future generations to produce the same value output that is consumed by the present generation. This would require depleted renewable resources to be renewed, and nonrenewable resources to be conserved, with the expectation that substitutes can eventually be found for them. Sustainability would also require that the capacity to assimilate waste would eventually reach an equilibrium with the amount of waste created. This sustainability standard could be met by modern industrial countries where technological advances will undoubtedly increase natural resource productivity to permit a rising per capita income. But even this standard may not be possible for many developing countries to achieve where substantial destruction of the resource base is taking place.

Maintaining sufficient natural resources to provide a constant per capita output for all countries

A constant per capita output standard would pose no insoluble problems for industrial countries, but would be impossible for many developing countries to achieve without a sharp reduction in the population growth rate, or substantial emigration, or by large and continuing transfers of financial resources from the industrial countries. Much of the current consumption by the poorest countries consists of resource depletion – forests, soil, minerals, water, and biodiversity – which could not continue if a constant per capita output were to be maintained. Bringing this depletion to a halt will require large investments in resource restoration and changes in current production practices. Unless financed by capital imports, these investments would be at the expense of consumption until productivity is raised.

It is sometimes argued that the industrial countries have an obligation to limit per capita output growth, or even decrease their present consumption of goods and services, to permit the developing world – which contains three-fourths of the world's population – to maintain or increase their real per capita income. This argument is based on the assumption that industrial countries are depleting the world's natural resources at a rate that may leave insufficient supplies for developing countries. This assumption also applies to the degradation of the global environment. But if the industrial world eliminated its negative impact on the global environment and adopted conditions for sustainable development with a rising per capita income achieved through technological advance, would the industrial world be consuming so much of the world's natural resources that the developing countries would be unable to increase per capita output, or even to maintain present per capita output, given a near doubling of the population in the developing countries over the next 35 years?

One way of answering these questions is to estimate how much nonfuel minerals and energy the world would require if per capita gross domestic product (GDP) in all countries grew at an annual rate of 3 percent over the next half century, and to relate these estimates to a projection of world supplies of these resources. If it were found that supplies would be insufficient to meet total demand at current nonfuel mineral and energy prices, the industrial countries could command much of the available natural resources by bidding up their prices to levels beyond the purchasing power of most developing countries. For developing countries to be able to grow, therefore, the industrial countries would need to curtail their demand for these resources and, consequently, their per capita GDP growth (Gordon *et al.,* 1987). This analysis assumes that in the absence of constraints on world supplies of these resources at current prices, the developing world could increase per capita GDP by 3 percent per annum. But there are other constraints on their growth in per capita output. These include the low rate of saving in poor countries, the limitations of their natural resources in the form of productive land and water, and their low rate of productivity growth. Also, it is possible that more abundant substitutes for scarce nonfuel minerals and new cheap sources of energy will be found, so that the principal natural resource constraints on growth in developing countries may be their own soil and water.

There is considerable difference of opinion among resource economists as to whether nonfuel minerals and energy will ever become so scarce as to cause a substantial long-term rise in their real prices. The technological optimists believe that more abundant substitutes will be found to prevent such a scarcity from limiting world GDP growth. Moreover, since a large proportion of the nonfuel minerals and petroleum comes from the developing countries themselves, some of them would benefit from an increase in prices for these resources. Thus, the argument used by some environmental economists that continued growth of minerals and energy consumption by the industrial countries is a barrier to growth by the developing countries is a gross oversimplification and subject to question.

When we turn to natural resources that are not traded internationally, such as agricultural topsoil, regional water supplies, and forests needed to preserve watersheds, more difficult issues arise. All nations following a sustainable development path must preserve their natural resources through conservation and renewal, but the failure of a large part of the world to do so will eventually raise world prices for foods and fibers, and all nations import a portion of their requirements. Also, the failure of a large portion of the world to deal with air, water, and ground pollution will inevitably reduce world supplies of goods and services, spread pollution to other countries, and have an adverse impact on world health. The destruction of forests and wetlands and the pollution of lakes and rivers reduce wildlife habitat, including that for birds requiring a suitable global environment, so that the entire world loses amenity services. Clearly, all nations should protect the global commons by reducing greenhouse gases and chlorofluorocarbons (CFCs) to levels commensurate with the absorptive capacity of the upper atmosphere, by avoiding further pollution of oceans, and by preserving biodiversity – all of which affect the quality of life of all countries. Therefore, sustainability is a global problem and no nation is an island in the ecosystem. The failure of Brazil, or Mexico, or Nigeria, or India to adopt sustainability practices will impair the welfare of future generations of American, Japanese, and European residents.

Some environmentalists believe that world economic growth is already greatly limited by the ability of the earth and its atmosphere to absorb additional waste in the form of greenhouse gases, ozone-depleting CFCs, and toxic materials in the oceans, lakes, and rivers (Goodland, 1991, pp. 5–17). If this is true, industrial countries will need to stop growing to enable developing countries to grow out of poverty and achieve sustainable development. A more optimistic view, which I hold, is that technology and higher savings by the industrial countries can reduce the amount of waste going into the environment while at the same time enabling them to produce higher levels of per capita output. Since a large transfer of wealth from the industrial countries to the poor countries and the abandoning of growth are politically impossible, they had better try to move along the path of continuing growth while moderating their impacts on the national and global environment. This means that the industrial world must meet its rising demand for energy by developing energy from nonpolluting sources, such as solar energy, the enormous sources of heat below the earth's crust, or relatively safe forms of nuclear energy, such as fusion.

National versus global sustainability

Given the global nature of sustainability, what are the conditions for international sustainable development? We may begin by imagining a world economic union in which all resource and environmental policies are formulated and implemented by a world authority. Let us assume that the objective of the hypothetical world authority is to maximize world 'net social output' (social output of goods and services less social costs of natural resource depletion or damage), subject to the constraint that there can be no net reduction in the value of the natural resource base. If we assume free trade in goods and services and free mobility of capital, labor and enterprise, inevitably some regions will grow faster than others. Some regions with degraded natural resources, or with natural resources that would contribute more to the global economy if left in a natural state, might not experience any growth. However, differences in per capita income arising from sustainability measures would tend to be adjusted mainly by movements of labor and capital among the regions.

Let us assume that this world economic authority, dedicated to maximizing the net social product while preserving the value of the natural resource base for future generations, would be able to apply on a global scale the same economic instruments as a national economic authority. The world economic authority would need to institute a variety of taxation and fiscal measures designed to conserve exhaustible natural resources, to renew or otherwise maintain the value of renewable resources, and to promote recycling, pollution abatement, and waste management practices to prevent producing more waste materials than global capacity could assimilate. In implementing the conditions for sustainability, the world authority would be using least-cost methods, since otherwise it could not maximize the net social output. Therefore, the authority would not favor one region over another by, say, requiring one region to meet more rigorous environmental and resource conservation standards than another. Distributional equity would not be an objective in carrying out sustainability, so that poor nations would not be favored over rich ones. However, the world authority might be empowered to use measures, such as taxation of net incomes and the distribution of fiscal revenues, for achieving greater distributional equity, as long as these measures did not significantly impair sustainability or reduce the net social output.

The reader will perceive many problems in this hypothetical scenario. However, the purpose is to provide a model for world sustainable development under a single authority that we can compare to an aggregation of national economic policies, all designed to achieve national sustainable development. Even if there were a desire on the part of all national governments to achieve global sustainability, national economic policies would be likely to fall far short of achieving the same collective result that could be realized by a world economic authority.

One reason is that national governments could not adopt the objective of maximizing world net social output. Nations seek to maximize national welfare, even when they contribute economic assistance to poorer countries. The justification is usually promotion of an economic and/or political advantage to the donor country. Famines, earthquakes, and typhoons resulting in large-scale human suffering will induce humanitarian aid, but this aid is only temporary and not in response to a desire for international equity. National self-interest also limits the willingness of countries to assist others in achieving a condition of sustainability, except where it is in the donor's interest to do so. It is easy to show an interest in particular measures, such as assisting a Latin American country to preserve its tropical forests, but this does not constitute a paradigm for a program of global sustainability. Every nation realizes it will be harmed by a deterioration of the global environment. However, taking unilateral action to protect the global environment at a considerable economic cost will not provide commensurate benefits, unless all or most countries take the same action. Agreements on ocean fisheries, greenhouse gases, and CFCs are difficult to negotiate and more difficult to implement. The problem is often complicated by disagreements among governments as to the probability and extent of global harm that will actually occur, and by differing perceptions of how global harm will be distributed among nations.

Finally, a national commitment to sustainable development will be largely confined to the resources of the nation or possibly to regions within nations. If one nation seeks to preserve its forests, it will import more lumber from (or export less lumber to) other countries, so there may be little contribution to sustaining world forests. Even if there is an agreement among the world's resource economists that there should be global conservation of a number of exhaustible resources, including energy, the fact that nearly all nations are either net exporters or net importers of some of these resources renders an international agreement on taxation or other conservation measures virtually impossible to achieve. Let us take a key commodity – petroleum. Assuming that energy specialists could agree on an optimum global consumption path for petroleum, it is unlikely that diverse national interests could reach an agreement on a global program to realize this path.

For these reasons, a collection of national policies for sustainable development could never approach the potential results of a hypothetical world economic authority. The success of national sustainable development policies will depend in large measure on obtaining international agreements to protect the global environment, but such agreements tend to compromise competing national positions rather than to achieve globally optimal solutions.

Resource Accounting

Traditional national product accounting treats the revenue from harvesting trees and mining ore as part of the net national product. Yet as buildings and machinery deteriorate with use, the reduction in their value is treated as depreciation and subtracted from the net national product. Resource accounting corrects this discriminatory treatment by treating depletion and deterioration of natural resource capital as capital consumption. It includes any loss of value of natural resources caused by human production, including pollution of water and the atmosphere and the deterioration of the soil used in agriculture.

A proper method of measuring the national product or national income is essential for understanding and measuring sustainable development. Sir John Hicks (1946, p. 172) stated that true income is the maximum value that an individual can consume during a time period and still be as well off at the end of the period as at the beginning. When we apply this concept to a nation or to the world, it implies that consumption should be limited over a given period to an amount that will leave the nation or world as well off at the end of the period as it was at the beginning.

Two types of adjustment of the net national product have been suggested for measuring sustainable income. The first is the deduction of the depletion of natural capital, including both nonrenewable and renewable resources. Damage to the global environment, such as accumulation of greenhouse gases, depletion of the ozone layer, and pollution of the oceans, should also be deducted, but no social cost estimates are available. The argument for deducting depletion of natural resources is that such depletion is consuming natural capital, analogous to consuming inventories of food and materials, or the depreciation on buildings and machinery. A second suggested deduction is 'defensive' expenditures, such as those for environmental protection, and for compensating environmental damage, for example medical expenses for people whose health is impaired by toxins in the air, water, or land. The argument for deducting 'defensive' expenditures is that they provide no net utilities; they only compensate for or avoid disutilities associated with production.

There are problems in estimating depletion of mineral reserves since known reserves are not static and tend to increase with exploration and technological advances for extracting lower-grade minerals. For example, known reserves of copper and petroleum are many times larger today than they were one hundred years ago, and for many minerals known reserves are rising faster than current extraction. Also, technological developments make it possible to substitute more abundant minerals for scarce ones. If in the next 50 years nuclear fusion and cheap methods of producing solar power are developed, our sources of energy could meet almost any conceivable future demand. On the other hand, many developing countries are rapidly depleting their productive soil and sources of water. Although there is an abundance of water in the oceans, the cost of desalinization is many times the cost of diverting rivers to irrigation and household use (Ahmad *et al.*, 1989).

What are the advantages of using resource accounting? Policy makers in all countries would have more accurate knowledge of national economic performance. What may appear to be good performance on the basis of conventional national product growth may be much less satisfactory if a country is depleting its natural resource base. The nonmarket data generated by estimating natural resource depletion provide important information for economic planning since such deterioration will affect the country's potential for future growth. A country that is a large producer and exporter of natural resources needs to be aware of how the exhaustion of its reserves will affect its output and income in the future. For example, a study of the Indonesian economy (Repetto *et al.*, 1989, p. 4) shows that while that country's GDP increased at an average annual rate of 7.1 percent from 1971 to 1984, the net domestic product, after allowance for depletion of petroleum reserves and timber stocks, and for soil erosion (based on loss of agricultural productivity), rose by only 4.0 percent per year. The estimates of annual resource depletion given in this study are net figures, the difference between annual additions and annual extractions or losses. Thus, new discoveries of petroleum reserves and replanted trees are additions to natural resources. It is also possible to restore soil productivity by growing grasses instead of crops.

As countries spend more on environmental protection, a larger share of their gross output must go for 'defensive' expenditures, which provide neither real output for consumption nor investment for growth. Although countries must increase these 'defensive' expenditures to maintain or restore the quality of life and prevent further deterioration of their natural resource base, policy makers should be aware of the impact of these expenditures on future levels of living and investment. For some countries, this may require a substantial increase in the savings rate if per capita consumption is to be maintained.

Because a large portion of developing countries output is resource intensive and most exports have a high natural resource value (minerals or agricultural products), resource accounting is especially important for Third World countries. A number of developing countries heavily dependent on mineral exports will exhaust these resources early in the next century unless additional reserves are found. They need to save a sufficient portion of the revenue from the resource industries to reinvest in nonresource industries, such as manufacturing, to maintain their net national product after the mineral resources are exhausted. Currently not enough of their revenue is saved because total revenue, including natural resource depletion, is regarded as available for consumption.

Probably the greatest loss of natural capital in the poorest developing countries is the loss of productive soil. This occurs in part because heavy deforestation has promoted flooding and water runoff, which have carried away topsoil. Overgrazing and improper crop production have also caused erosion and loss of nutrients from the soil. Improperly managed irrigation systems have resulted in soil salinization, waterlogging, and heavy sedimentation of rivers below the irrigated areas. Every year sub-Saharan African countries lose millions of acres of agricultural land and, despite large amounts of fertilizer, remaining soils are losing their productivity. This is an enormous loss of natural resource capital, but it can be stemmed, and to some extent reversed, by changing farming and grazing practices and by investing in the land, including rehabilitation of existing irrigation systems. These actions will divert considerable output from current consumption, the impacts of which need to be taken into account by policy makers. Resource accounting should also be used by multilateral development banks and bilateral aid agencies to enable them to assess the performance of their clients and to advise and assist them in planning for the future.

Most economists object to abandoning the traditional national product accounts in favor of resource accounting. Information available for measuring the depletion and deterioration of natural resources over a given period is sparse and imprecise, and the methods of measurement are subject to considerable controversy. Therefore, most environmental economists favor constructing 'satellite' resource accounts, which can be linked to the current accounting systems for certain purposes, rather than replacing the current system. Thus, in the study of the Indonesian economy referred to above, the estimates of the reduction in annual petroleum reserves, timber stocks, and the annual soil erosion could be listed in a 'satellite' resource account. To this account should be added estimates of the annual 'defensive' environmental expenditures which were made or *should have been made* for pollution abatement or for other types of environmental protection. This 'satellite' account can be used to adjust the GDP to show the net domestic product after allowance for resource depletion and 'defensive' expenditures.

How the Sustainability Criterion Affects Development Policy

It is sometimes argued that poor countries are under such pressure to eliminate poverty that they cannot afford to devote their labor and capital to environmental protection and natural resource conservation. Therefore, they must concentrate on economic growth and defer efforts to protect the environment until they have higher per capita incomes. Such an argument is analogous to running a factory seven days a week, week after week, without any outlays for maintenance. Inevitably there will come a time when the factory must shut down completely and perhaps be faced with a large outlay for major repairs or replacements, at a far larger cost than if maintenance had taken place on a regular basis. But society is, of course, more than a machine producing goods and services. It should seek to maximize social welfare, and maximizing social well-being is what distinguishes development as an objective from that of maximizing per capita GDP. Unlike economic growth, development progress cannot be measured by a single indicator. There is no agreement on the value content of development, nor on what combination of indexes should be used to measure social welfare. In a democratic society, what constitutes social welfare is determined by the collective desires of the people and is expressed by how people choose to allocate their incomes, and by the policies of the governments they elect and support.

Some of what we call sustainability has always been included in economic development objectives – the elimination of public exposure to environmental hazards and preservation of forests and scenic rivers for recreation. What is added by the concept of sustainable development is the maintenance and enhancement of the natural resource base and its productivity for the benefit of both present and future generations. As in the case of other development objectives, the concern for future generations is a social value whose relative importance as a development objective is determined by social demand. Placing a high value on utilities enjoyed by future generations is contrary to the almost universal tendency of individuals to discount future goods. This is evidenced by the fact that people are willing to pay interest in order to have homes, automobiles and other durable goods now, rather than waiting until they can pay cash for them. Also, we are accustomed to expecting that future generations will have more and better goods and services per capita than our own, but as natural resources become more scarce this pattern may not continue.

The traditional basis for valuing natural resources is the present (discounted) value of the annual income from their use in producing goods and services. Since future income from extracting petroleum or copper is discounted, their value to future generations, say, one living 50 years from now, is only a small fraction of their value today. Yet 50 years from now their value to that generation is likely to be much higher than the value we give to these natural resources today. Herein lies the heart of the problem of conserving natural resources for the use of future generations: consuming natural resources today has a much higher value than conserving them for future generations; the further in the future the goods are consumed, the lower the value they will have today.

How can we induce the present generation to put a higher value on goods and services to be consumed well into the future? Parents and grandparents will often save for their children, but they are unlikely to sacrifice much of their present consumption for great-grandchildren they may never see. Some environmental economists have suggested that we use a lower rate of discount for valuing natural resources. But almost any positive rate of discount will place a minuscule value on natural resources available to a generation living 100 years from now. Also, it is illogical to use one rate of discount for valuing natural resources and another for valuing man-made goods and services. The decision to conserve natural resources for the use of future generations is a social decision, not a private one. If the present generation decides it has a moral responsibility to pass on to future generations a natural resource base of value equal to that which the present generation inherited from the past, only the government, which usually regards itself as a government of the future as well as present, can carry out this mandate. This does not mean that the government should take title to and control of all natural resources, but the government can by means of taxation and economic incentives carry out a program of natural resource conservation and renewal.

Although sustainable development alters and broadens development objectives, most of the traditional theory and analysis remains relevant. The specification of the production functions, the contribution of capital to growth, the effects of technological progress, the effectiveness of various types of economic incentives on production, investment and saving, and the effects of monetary, fiscal, foreign exchange, and trade policies on demand, investment, and production are not significantly altered from conventional economic development. There will, of course, be changes in development priorities, with greater emphasis on preserving and restoring nonrenewable resources and conserving exhaustible ones. Nonmonetary social costs and benefits will play a larger role in social benefit–cost analysis of particular projects and programs. In the production process, the choice of inputs and of technologies will take into account environmental costs, including the global effects.

Sustainability criteria complicate economic analysis by requiring the determination of monetary equivalents for nonmonetary social benefits and costs associated with all economic activity. Many governmental projects, such as roads, municipal water systems, waste disposal and sanitation projects, and the creation of parks and wildlife refuges, provide social benefits that are not paid for by individual users, or at least the users do not pay the full costs of the services. Some of the costs involved in providing these services are environmental costs, such as pollution and the depletion of natural resources. It is not sufficient simply to identify the nonmonetary impacts; the impacts must be assigned monetary values. If a government or a private organization is considering constructing a multipurpose dam for irrigation and generation of hydropower, it is not enough to determine the economic feasibility of the project by calculating the monetary costs of operating and constructing the dam, and comparing these costs with the revenues from the power and additional agricultural output. It is necessary to estimate the full costs to the people forced to evacuate the lands flooded by the reservoir created by the dam; the costs to the communities downstream from the dam from sedimentation and pollution of the river generated by the irrigated area; and the costs of the loss of forests resulting from dam construction and the erection of power transmission lines. Many of the costs that should be added to the social costs of a dam are nonmonetary and must be monetarized, so that they may be compared with the social benefits from the project.

The environmental costs for all industrial and agricultural projects need to be estimated and internalized by the project producers. This means the costs must be paid by the producers, which will induce them to avoid or mitigate the adverse environmental costs in an effective way. The internalized costs will, of course, be passed on by the producers to the users in the form of higher prices, since otherwise the projects would not be undertaken. If it is determined that the social costs exceed what society is willing to pay for them, the project should not be undertaken. This approach, which is inherent in sustainable development, will revolutionize benefit–cost accounting and the evaluation of public and private projects.

Project Evaluation and Selection

Sustainable development is not achieved by policy statements of government officials or by officials of the World Bank. Sustainability must be embodied in particular projects and programs, and in the criteria for evaluating and selecting projects. Since projects and programs have important impacts on future economic behavior, it is easier to introduce sustainable development practices into new projects than into the operation of old ones. Therefore, we need to examine more closely how governments and foreign assistance agencies should evaluate proposed projects from the standpoint of their compatibility with sustainable development.

Although it is not possible to embody all the attributes of sustainable development in a single project or program, it should be possible to design a project that is consistent with the sustainability of the value of the natural resources used in the project. This means that the productivity of the resource would be maintained over time, either by renewing the resource or by investing in other capital assets an amount equal to the capital value of that portion of the resource that has been depleted by the construction and operation of the project. This sustainability criterion is satisfied by including in the social cost of the project any reduction in the value of the resource caused by depletion or degradation. This would include not only the natural resource used in the project, but any adverse effects on the natural resource base. Thus a project that significantly reduces the productivity of the land, or the quality of the atmosphere, rivers, or lakes gives rise to social costs.

Whether a development project or program should be undertaken or approved for support by an external assistance agency should normally depend upon its net present social value (NPSV). The use of a particular natural resource, whether for development or for preservation, should be determined by which use yields the highest NPSV, and, in any case, development should not be undertaken where the NPSV is not positive. To embody the principle of sustainable development into the process of project evaluation, any resource depletion arising directly or indirectly from the project should be treated as a social cost in calculating the NPSV. Thus, a project that involves a large amount of natural resource depletion will tend to have a lower NPSV than one that has little impact on natural resources.

If natural resource depletion is treated as a social cost in project evaluation, a twofold problem arises. How do you measure the value of the depletion and how much revenue do you need to save and reinvest to maintain the same income (after allowance for depletion) for future generations? The revenue from a resource project that is attributed to the natural resource is the total receipts from sale of the products, less the associated capital and labor costs. We may divide this revenue, R, into two components: the income component, X, and the capital component, $R - X$, representing the natural resource depletion. We need to define $R - X$ so that it can be used as a social cost in calculating NPSV. How $R - X$ is determined can best be shown by the following example.[2]

Let us assume we have a mining project with annual gross receipts, R. Assume the mine fully depletes in n years, and that each year a portion of the revenue, $R - X$, is saved and invested to allow for depletion, leaving X as income for the mine owners. For sustainability of the resource, $R - X$ should be sufficient to accumulate a fund that would enable the owners to receive an infinite series of X, assuming a constant rate of interest, r.

In order to accumulate this fund, annual depletion $(R - X)$ must be an amount which when reinvested at r each year for n years will provide an accumulated sum at the end of n years sufficient to yield an annual income of X. To take a numerical example, assume R is \$250,000 (all monetary values in this book are in US dollars) per year, the life of the mine is 20 years, and the rate of interest is 10 percent. Annual depletion equals \$37,000, which when saved and compounded at 10 percent over twenty years equals \$2,130,000. This amount yields annual income (X) of \$213,000 in perpetuity. The longer the life of the mine and the higher the rate of interest, the smaller the proportion of R that needs to be saved for depletion. For a mine that depletes in ten years, and assuming an interest rate of 5 percent, 75 percent of R would need to be saved for depletion. This compares with 15 percent in the first example.

The NPSV of the mine is the present value of the annual stream, R, minus the present value of annual depletion $(R - X)$, or the present value of X. Assuming R is $250,000, the NPSV for a mine with a life of 20 years and a rate of interest of 10 percent is about $1.8 million. With higher annual depletion, the NPSV is much smaller. Thus, for a mine with a life of only ten years, depletion is 35 percent of R, as against 15 percent of R in the first example.

We may generalize the analysis given above by stating that the NPSV of a project, with allowance for resource depletion, is the present value of an annual stream, R, minus the present value of RD, where RD is the average annual resource depletion during the life of the project. The actual resource depletion might take place at any time rather than in equal amounts over the life of the project. However, to satisfy the resource sustainability criterion, it makes little difference to future generations when the actual depletion takes place during the life of a project. Resource depletion need not be confined to the depletion of reserves in a mining project. It may take the form of environmental damage caused by a mine or by any other project that reduces the productivity of natural resources. For example, a mining operation might pollute a river, thereby reducing the value of the fish catch. The present value of the loss of fish catch would be a part of the social cost of the mine, thereby lowering the NPSV of the project. Alternatively, a hydroelectric dam might cause environmental damage to the recreational value of a river. If the damage were substantial, RD might be so large as to make the NPSV of the project very low or negative, in which case it would not be financed by an external agency.

In calculating NPSV, there should be an allowance for risk made by applying probability coefficients to each of the relevant variables. In this way it is possible to estimate the *expected* NPSV of the project.

Reinvesting the resource depletion

In the approach to project evaluation outlined above, it makes no difference whether the accumulated depreciation is reinvested for renewing the depleted resource or used for some other capital improvement, as long as the investment yields a net social output equal to that lost by resource depletion. The paradigm is the reinvestment of the depreciation of a building or a machine. If a project destroys an old growth forest or part of a scenic river, the reduced value of the resource as a producer of utilities should be compensated by an investment that will yield a stream of utilities equal to that which was lost. The investment may take the form of restoring the depleted natural resource, creating man-made physical capital, or improving human knowledge and skills for increasing the productivity of the resource base.

Three problems arise in rendering the above model consistent with sustainability. First, changing the system of accounting to include resource depletion as a social cost will not necessarily induce private entities to save and reinvest social capital. Private firms and individuals may still treat natural resource depletion as income available for consumption and, except for depletion allowances for some types of natural resource exploitation, the tax system will count resource depletion as taxable income. Therefore, sustainability will require resource depletion to be taxed by the state and reinvested in a manner that will sustain output for future generations. The tax will, of course, be passed on to consumers. The prices of goods whose production involves heavy resource depletion will be relatively higher than that of those involving less depletion. The state could either invest the revenues directly, or use the revenues to induce private investment for increasing the social product.

The second problem is to determine which social investments made or induced by the state will insure that future generations receive the capitalized value of the resources depleted by the present generation. Suppose that most of the tax revenue is invested in roads and buildings rather than in restoring depleted renewable natural resources or increasing the productivity of natural resources. How far can we go in substituting man-made physical capital for natural resource capital and still maintain a rising national or world output? We cannot assume that aggregate national or world production is a Cobb–Douglas production function, in which the productive factors are completely substitutable. Herman Daly (1991) argues that the substitutability of man-made capital for natural resources is quite limited. In other words, unless the raw material base is maintained, long-run sustainability is impossible. This position is highly controversial and some resource economists believe that we can offset considerable resource depletion by increasing the productivity of natural resource capital. This question is considered in Chapter 8. In any case, sustainability requires that a substantial amount of the resource depletion be invested in replenishing renewable resources, in increasing product output per unit of resource input, or in increasing the end-use efficiency of resource-intensive products.

A third problem concerns substitutability on the demand side. How far can we go in satisfying the demand for wilderness amenities, clean air, and living space with man-made goods? There is surely a point beyond which further degradation of the environment cannot be compensated by higher per capita real income in the form of produced goods and services. What is the utility trade-off in driving a Cadillac or Mercedes in a perpetual traffic jam surrounded by foul air against walking through a grove of ancient redwoods? There are also limits on the extent to which we can allow the natural environment to deteriorate and still survive as a species.

Technological progress can offset depletion of the resource base by increasing the productivity of the remaining resources. It can also facilitate the substitution of man-made capital assets for natural resources and the substitution of more abundant for scarce natural resources in production. However, with a rising population, technological progress is necessary to maintain or increase per capita utilities for future generations. There are two reasons for not including technological progress in the calculation of the social costs represented by the depletion of the resource base. First, we do not know enough about future technology to assess its impact on the productivity of the resources used in particular projects. Second, we should allow technological progress to have its full effect on improving the well-being of future generations. Therefore, the social cost of the depletion of natural resources attributable to a project should be based on current technology.

Criteria for MDB-supported projects

For a project to qualify for support from a multilateral development bank, the *expected* NPSV adjusted for resource depletion should be positive. The expected NPSV of a proposed project *without allowance for resource depletion* is frequently regarded as *resource rent* (Mikesell, 1989). If resource rent is zero, the resource contributes nothing to social output, since the labor, capital, and management included in the social costs could produce the same value output in another project without using natural resources. However, for a project to satisfy the condition of sustainability, the resource rent must be at least equal to the resource depletion caused directly or indirectly by construction and operation of the project. If the *expected* NPSV adjusted for resource depletion were zero, the resource used would contribute nothing to net revenue, and it would probably be better to leave it undeveloped. This would be true for a wilderness area that could be used by fishermen and hikers as an alternative to harvesting the timber at a zero or negative NPSV. Also, the alternative of leaving the resource undisturbed would have an additional value, which is called *reversibility*. When resources are not disturbed they can always be developed at some time in the future when the need for the products of the project is greater. This value is in addition to the possible amenities yielded by resources left in their natural state. Ideally, the resource use providing the maximum expected NPSV should be supported. Frequently, that means simply leaving the resource in an undeveloped state.

How Sustainable Development Might Influence Development Priorities in the Allocation of Capital in Developing Countries

In traditional development theory, capital should be allocated with a view to maximizing the long-run financial return on investments. This criterion is also consistent with maximizing labor income and the national product, since the most profitable industries will bid labor away from less profitable ones, and wages will be higher where productivity is greatest. Productivity will also be enhanced by profits reinvested in research and development (R&D), with a consequent increase in per capita income. With free domestic and international trade, a nation will be led to specialize in those goods and services in which it has a comparative advantage. The most profitable industries will also attract capital from abroad, provided political and economic conditions are stable. A government can promote this pattern of resource allocation by providing the infrastructure required by industries growing in response to the most profitable opportunities. In the case of developing countries, external assistance from the MDBs should support the infrastructure requirements of the more profitable industries, and sometimes the industries themselves. Of course, external assistance agencies have other objectives, such as reducing poverty and providing a variety of social services, but the bulk of their assistance for promoting growth goes to support those economic activities with the greatest long-run potential of profitability and expansion.

How might adherence to the principles of sustainable development change the pattern of resource allocation? Many countries need to allocate more resources to pollution abatement, especially in their cities. This is taking place in the industrial countries, but is lagging in Eastern Europe and in large Third World municipalities. In Eastern European countries, industrial pollution has contributed heavily to low productivity and was one of the reasons for the failure of their socialist systems. In many Third World countries, air, water, and land pollution are so serious that productivity and the quality of life are impaired. Water pollution is limiting supplies of water available to industry and agriculture. Very large amounts of capital will be required for industrial pollution abatement and, in some cases, entirely new plants need to be built. In addition, industrial firms need to be moved out of large cities and into smaller communities.

In the rural areas, measures should be taken to reduce the contamination of rivers, lakes, and irrigation canals by fertilizers, pesticides, and household wastes; and irrigation systems need to be overhauled for the more efficient use of water and to avoid salinization and waterlogging. Given the limited supply of capital, all of these measures will require a reduction in capital outlays for certain types of infrastructure and for private durable goods, such as cars. Sustainable development in agriculture calls for fewer and smaller irrigation dams in favor of replacing old systems, and multipurpose dams should make agriculture rather than power their primary function.

In addition to affecting the allocation of investment, sustainable development considerations may alter the directions which development takes in terms of sectoral priorities. A good example is provided in an unpublished study of the implications of long-run water resource availability in Egypt. Egypt's development planning has emphasized the expansion of irrigated areas for the production of cotton and other export commodities. But a projection of the demand for water indicates an excess of demand over supply early in the next century. Water in the Egyptian Nile is vulnerable to the use of the Nile and its tributaries by countries to the south. The study recommends that Egypt shift to producing industrial commodities as a means of expanding exports and relying less on Nile-dependent agriculture. Also, Egypt needs to conserve water by changing irrigation methods and by avoiding pollution. Conservation could be encouraged by metering water for irrigation and charging prices approximating long-run marginal costs. In addition to water conservation through more efficient use, reduced production of water-intensive crops and a shift from irrigated to rain-fed agriculture may be dictated by long-run supply conditions. Such adjustments should be achieved by increasing the price of water to reflect long-run demand and supply conditions.

In a number of developing countries, a shortage of fertile land has encouraged landless people to move to upland areas with poor soil and to tropical forests, where the trees are destroyed to provide land for crops and cattle grazing. These movements have been encouraged by governments through subsidizing migration and converting forested and marginal land to agricultural uses. This has often proved costly. Because of serious erosion, the marginal land produces little output and the deforested area becomes unsuitable for farming after only a few crops. Valuable watershed is impaired and there is a loss of the nonforest products of tropical forest areas. It has been shown that more intensive farming of better quality agricultural land is more cost-effective than short-term increases in output in marginal and forested areas.

Very often the prices for resource inputs do not promote the optimum long-term use of the resources. In many cases this is because of improper governmental pricing of water and other resources, but in other cases the operation of free markets for resources does not result in prices that induce sustainability. Market imperfections and government-controlled prices that undervalue resources increase the current demand for those resources to levels far greater than required for sustainability. Governments can correct these conditions by appropriate pricing polices and the use of taxes to raise the prices of resources in line with their long-run values.

Effects of Environmental Externalities on Production

Some economic activities impair other economic activities that produce a greater value output. These effects, which we call externalities, have long been recognized in economic theory, but the environmental movement has made economists more conscious of them and of the need to take account of the external impacts of resource industries. The following case history illustrates how one resource industry may damage another.

Bacuit Bay on the island of Palawan in the Philippines has in recent years become an important fishing area, and has also attracted an increasing number of scuba divers to its clear water and coral. In January 1985, logging operations bordering Bacuit Bay commenced, only to be temporarily suspended the following year. The principal impact of logging is erosion, created by the soil disturbance from logging and road building in the area. Erosion resulted in a flow of sediment into the Manlag River that drains into Bacuit Bay. Since Palawan has high annual rainfall, a large amount of sediment from logging operations is brought into the Bay, thereby reducing the clarity of the water and destroying the coral. This reduces the attractiveness of the water for divers and other tourists, and has an adverse effect on the fish catch.

A conflict over the impact of logging on fishing and tourism led to a study by the East–West Environment and Policy Institute (Hudgson and Dixon, 1988, p. 57). This study estimated the capitalized value of the revenues under two development options for the Bacuit Bay drainage basin: Option 1, all logging is banned in the Bacuit Bay drainage basin forest area; or Option 2, logging continues within the Bacuit Bay drainage basin forest area. The analysis was done on a gross revenue basis for tourism, fisheries, and logging under the two options. Two discount rate assumptions – 10 and 15 percent – were used to determine present values. The resulting present value calculations are sensitive to the rate of discount used since revenue from logging is realized within a relatively short period of time, while revenues from fisheries and tourism have a lower annual average, but continue indefinitely – with revenue from tourism expected to increase significantly over time.

The study found that the capitalized value of gross revenues from tourist income and the fish catch for Option 1 (using a 10 percent discount rate) is almost double the capitalized value of the gross revenue under Option 2. Since all logging under Option 2 occurs during the first five years, the effect of using a 15 percent discount rate on the present value of gross revenue generated from logging is relatively slight, but it does reduce the present value of the tourist and fishing revenues. However, even at the higher 15 percent discount rate, the total present value of gross revenue under Option 1 is still 1.5 times higher than that under Option 2 (Hudgson and Dixon, 1988, pp. 58–9).

These calculations do not take account of intergenerational equity or sustainability of output. Once the trees are harvested, the revenues from logging are gone until new trees become available from reforestation. However, the next generation will experience a significant loss in tourism and fishery revenues. Therefore, the nonlogging option favors intergenerational equity and sustainability. In addition, there are ecological consequences from logging, such as the loss of wildlife habitat and biological diversity, that need to be taken into account in a comprehensive analysis.

Can There Be Both Sustainability and Growth?

Early nineteenth-century economists, such as Thomas Malthus (1766–1834) and David Ricardo (1771–1823), were pessimistic about prospects for long-term economic growth, despite a surge in industrial productivity beginning in the late eighteenth century, and the increase in agricultural land available for producing foods and fibers in the New World. The world was not accustomed to growth, and increases in per capita output were barely discernible in Europe until the nineteenth century. Growth pessimism was based on the scarcity of natural resources and the absence of restraints other than limited food supply on population growth. Growth pessimism and the belief that mankind could never escape from the low income trap, because any significant rise in per capita income would be annulled by population growth, earned for economics the appellation of 'dismal science.' In the late nineteenth and early twentieth centuries this pessimism was replaced by optimism based on the expectation of continual technological progress and the adoption of birth control in the industrial countries. This growth optimism was substantiated by the remarkable growth in per capita output in the industrial countries and in many Third World countries as well (especially Latin America and East Asia). But by the 1970s rates of growth in per capita output began to decline in nearly all countries except Japan, and there was a decline in per capita output in Africa. In the 1980s only a few Third World countries had significant per capita growth. Currently there is concern about the effects of the deterioration of the global environment on the future productivity and livability of the earth. Growth pessimism has again become popular and many environmentalists are challenging growth as the major objective of long-run economic policy. An important question, therefore, is whether we can have both sustainability and growth as realistic goals.

The authors of the well-known book, *The Limits to Growth* (Meadows *et al.*, 1972), argued that the developed world will need to stop growing if there are to be enough natural resources for the developing world to survive. This position was associated with a group known as the Club of Rome, whose report the book represented. This book sufficiently impressed the Carter

Administration for the President to appoint a committee which published an equally pessimistic outlook entitled *Global 2000 Report to the President* (1980), the major findings of which were:

> If present trends continue, the world in 2000 will be more crowded, more polluted, less stable ecologically, and more vulnerable to disruption than the world we live in now. Serious stresses involving population, resources, and environment are clearly visible ahead. Despite greater material output, the world's people will be poorer in many ways than they are today.
>
> For hundreds of millions of the desperately poor, the outlook for food and other necessities of life will be no better. For many it will be worse. Barring revolutionary advances in technology, life for most people on earth will be more precarious in 2000 than it is now – unless the nations of the world act decisively to alter current trends.

In 1984 a number of prominent resource economists published a book entitled *The Resourceful Earth* (Simon and Kahn, 1984). The conclusion of this book is as follows:

> If present trends continue, the world in 2000 will be less crowded (though more populated), less polluted, more stable ecologically, and less vulnerable to resource-supply disruptions than the world we live in now. Stresses involving population, resources, and environment will be less in the future than now . . . the world's people will be richer in most ways than they are today . . . the outlook for food and other necessities of life will be better . . . life for most people will be less precarious economically than it is now.

The authors of this book, who are specialists in various resource categories, projected an optimistic outlook for food supply, the birth rate in developing countries, world forests, water, climate, mineral resources, and air and water pollution, and condemned the 'constraints currently imposed upon material progress by political and institutional forces, in conjunction with popularly-held beliefs and attitudes about natural resources and the environment, such as those urged upon us by *Global 2000*.'

In 1991 it was possible to discern in current trends verification for portions of both these assessments. For the developing countries as a group and for the world as a whole, per capita food production rose between 1979–81 and 1986–88, but for many of the poorest countries there was a decline. During the 1980s, population growth rates in developing countries, excluding China, did not decline below the 1965–80 rates. For many of these countries, limitations on land and water may preclude their maintaining current per capita food production, which is already barely at the subsistence level. Ecological conditions the world over have deteriorated, with a steady loss in biodiversity, mainly as a consequence of the rapid disappearance of primary tropical forests. The outlook for the global environment, especially the upper atmosphere, has deteriorated with the accumulation of greenhouse gases and the rapid depletion of ozone over the Antarctic. On the more hopeful side, technological progress has both increased supplies of and reduced our dependence on certain nonfuel minerals; energy sources have expanded in line with demand; and there has not been a rising trend in the real prices of either nonfuel minerals or energy as was predicted in the early 1970s. Perhaps the most hopeful development is the recognition of environmental problems and the need to do something about them. Aware- ness of the urgency of resource depletion by governments and by the bilateral and multilateral institutions providing economic assistance has been slow to arise, but it seems likely that the principles of sustainable development will be partially implemented in most Third World countries in the next decade or so. Political instability has probably worsened and could be a determining factor in whether sustainable policies are adopted by Third World governments.

Although the doomsday forecasts for the year 2000 will not come to pass, the outlook for human life by the year 2030, when world population will have doubled to nearly ten billion, is not optimistic – especially for the developing countries where more than 80 percent of the world's population will reside. Although some countries that adopt policies conducive to prod- uctivity, resource conservation, and foreign investment may well follow the path of South Korea and Taiwan, increasing poverty and starvation along with political instability and civil war in some countries may lead to condi- tions not yet imagined even by environmental pessimists.

Sustainable development is not premised on a no-growth condition, nor does it require that wealthy nations forgo per capita growth to permit developing countries to survive. Developed countries have an obligation to take the lead in halting the deterioration of the global environment, and to provide financial and technical assistance to developing countries where action to protect the global environment involves a considerable expense. But the position that countries with ample natural resources have an obliga- tion to transfer those resources or goods produced with them to resource- poor countries is not politically acceptable. It is in the interest of developed countries to assist poor countries to achieve sustainable development, but the ultimate responsibility for population control and for adopting economic policies conducive to sustainable development rests with the individual nations.

Summary

This chapter has shown how sustainable development economics sup- plements conventional analysis of development by the inclusion of the interaction between economic activity and the natural resource base com- posed of inputs to the production process and an absorber of waste generated by that process. Sustainable development also broadens conventional development objectives by including the preservation of the natural resource base to enable future generations to carry on at least an equivalent level of current economic activity. The national product should be adjusted downward for depletion of natural resources available for inputs and for the damage to the ability of the environment to absorb waste. Resource accounting should be applied to the evaluation of development projects and programs by deducting from their expected gross contribution to the social product the natural resource depletion and degradation associated with their formation and operation. However, given technological progress, environmental protection and resource conservation, sustainable development is not necessarily incompatible with economic growth in the traditional sense, either for present or for future generations. The special environmental and resource problems created by development projects and programs that may render them incompatible with sustainable development criteria are described in Chapter 3.

NOTES

1   For a compendium of definitions of sustainable development in the literature, see Pezzey (1989, Appendix 1).
2   This analysis is adopted from Mikesell (1991).

REFERENCES

Ahmad, Yusuf J., El Serafy, Salah and Lutz, Ernst (eds) (1989) *Environmental Accounting for Sustainable Development*. Washington, DC: World Bank.

Daly, Herman (1991) From empty-world to full-world economics: recognizing an historical turning point in economic development. In R. Goodland *et al.* (eds) *Environmentally Sustainable Economic Development: Building on Brundtland*, Environmental Working Paper no. 46. Washington, DC: World Bank.

Global 2000: Report to the President (1980) Washington, DC: US Government Printing Office.

Goodland, Robert (1991) Case that the world has reached limits: more precisely that current throughput growth in the global economy cannot be sustained. In R. Goodland *et al.* (eds) *Environmentally Sustainable Economic Development: Building on Brundtland*, Environmental Working Paper no. 46. Washington, DC: World Bank.

Gordon, Robert D., Koopmans, Tjalling C., Nordhaus, William D. and Skinner, Brian J. (1987) *Toward a New Iron Age: Quantitative Modeling of Resource Exhaustion*. Cambridge, MA: Harvard University Press.

Hicks, John R. (1946) *Value and Capital*, 2nd edn. Oxford: Oxford University Press.

Hudgson, Gregor and Dixon, John A. (1988) *Logging versus Fisheries and*

Tourism in Palawan: An Environmental and Economic Analysis. Honolulu, HI: University of Hawaii, East–West Center.

Meadows, Donella, Meadows, Dennis, Randers, Jorgen and Behrens, William, III (1972) *The Limits to Growth*. New York: Universe Books.

Mikesell, Raymond F. (1989) Depletable resources, discounting, and intergenerational equity. *Resources Policy*, December, 292–6.

Mikesell, Raymond F. (1991) Project evaluation and sustainable development. In R. Goodland *et al.* (eds), *Environmentally Sustainable Economic Development: Building on Brundtland*, Environmental Working Paper no. 46. Washington, DC: World Bank.

O'Riordan, Timothy (1988) The politics of sustainability. In R.K. Turner (ed.), *Sustainable Environment Management: Principles and Practice*. London: Belhaven Press.

Pezzey, John (1989) *Economic Analysis of Sustainable Growth and Sustainable Development*, Environmental Department Working Paper no. 15. Washington, DC: World Bank.

Repetto, Robert, Magrath, William, Wells, Michael, Beer, Christine and Rossini, Fabrizio (1989) *Wasting Assets: Natural Resources in the National Income Accounts*. Washington, DC: World Resources Institute.

Simon, Julian L. and Kahn, Herman (eds) (1984) *The Resourceful Earth*. New York: Basil Blackwell.

World Commission on Environment and Development (1987) *Our Common Future*. Oxford: Oxford University Press.

3

Environmental and Resource Problems Created by Development Projects

There are several categories of environmental and resource problems generated by development projects and programs. The most familiar is pollution of the atmosphere, water, or soil, which impairs the usefulness of these environmental assets for producing goods and services and/or creates disutilities for humans by causing illness and discomfort. A second category consists in destroying or altering natural resources in a manner that impairs their usefulness for more valuable economic activities or for providing direct utilities for humans. A good example is wasteful destruction of primary forests for conversion to cattle grazing. A third category of problems arises when projects or programs are designed or operated in such a way as to create unnecessary damage to natural resources or environment. There may be nothing wrong with the activities themselves, but the damage arises from the way the projects are designed or operated or from the activities they support. Examples include overgrazing and the use of agricultural methods causing soil loss or degradation. Irrigation systems are frequently operated in a way that causes waterlogging and salinity of the soil. The environmental harm done by these projects or activities is usually subject to correction by changes in the project and method of operation, and by better management.

The above three categories mainly affect the contemporary generation. A fourth category of resource problems arises from the violation of the principle of sustainability. A project may be justified in terms of social benefits exceeding social costs from the standpoint of the present generation, but the social benefits may not exceed social costs if the welfare of future generations is taken into account.[1] Natural resource depletion may take place slowly and not significantly affect the output or welfare of the present generation, but may seriously reduce the productive capacity and welfare of future generations. Examples include: a slow reduction in the fertility of the soil; a gradual decline in available groundwater; or a gradual disappearance of wildlife and biodiversity. On a global level, good examples are the accumulation of greenhouse gases and the depletion of organic life in the oceans.

Each of these four categories of resource and environmental problems is found in the major classifications of development projects analyzed in this chapter. All of these classes of projects are necessary for development, but the projects must meet certain standards to be consistent with sustainable development. In the following sections, the environmental impacts of major classes of development projects and programs are analyzed from the standpoint of both sustainable development and conventional development.

Industrialization and Urbanization

Traditional growth theory has identified growth with industrialization, and industrialization with the growth of cities. A popular hypothesis associated with W. Arthur Lewis (1954) is that growth is generated by a transfer of surplus labor in the rural sector to the industrial sector in the cities. This is made possible by capital investment financed by industrial profits, which are sustained as long as the supply of labor remains perfectly elastic at a wage determined by, but somewhat above, the subsistence level in the rural sector. Moreover, it is argued that since labor in the rural sector is in surplus, the transfer will not reduce agricultural output. Theodore Schultz (1964), Morton Paglin (1965), and others criticized the Lewis model, especially the assumption that the marginal productivity of labor in agriculture is zero. Development in most countries might have progressed faster if more capital had been invested in agriculture and fewer people had moved to the cities. Most environmental economists would agree with this assessment. However, the low- and middle-income developing countries appeared to have followed the path of rapid urbanization. Between 1965 and 1988 the percentage of the total population living in urban areas grew from 24 to 41 percent, and the percentage of the urban population in cities of over a half million persons grew from 31 to 44 percent. The number of cities with over half a million population rose from 110 to 278 (World Bank, 1990b, pp. 238–9). In sub-Saharan Africa, urban population as a percentage of total population rose from 14 to 28 percent, and the percentage of the urban population in cities of over half a million rose from 6 to 41 percent with the number of cities with over half a million population increasing from 3 to 28.

Since the Second World War the large metropolitan areas in the developing countries have become the most polluted in the world. Mexico City holds the world record for air pollution, Bombay for solid waste, and Manila for water pollution. Most of the investment in Third World countries has gone into urban areas, and, until recently, most of the external financial assistance has gone to support urban industry and infrastructure. Municipal waste and untreated sewage have long characterized the cities, but in recent decades air pollution and toxic effluents into waterways and the soil have become the most harmful sources of pollution. Added to these has been the growth in car and truck traffic in crowded metropolitan areas.

For the past quarter century there has been an expanding social demand for clean air, water, and land standards in the industrial countries, but demands for environmental reform have been weak in developing countries and in Eastern Europe. This has been caused in part by the overpowering emphasis by governments on growth that suppresses social demands in favor of the interests of bureaucracies, the military, and industrial leaders. In the Eastern European countries, industrial expansion and military capacity orchestrated by Moscow were almost the sole indicators of economic progress.

In the developing countries there has been little incentive to diversify industrial facilities outside the large cities. Power, transportation, and the labor supply are concentrated in large cities. Many environmental problems could have been averted by locating manufacturing operations in smaller communities, and by creating infrastructure and housing communities outside the metropolitan areas.

Concentration of industrialization is in part a consequence of the dominant role of government in large-scale production. In Third World countries, large state-owned enterprises did not evolve from small enterprises serving local or regional markets, as was frequently the pattern in industrial countries. Even where large enterprises are privately owned, the government often plays a major role in financing and in controlling competition to assure the profitability of the enterprise. The entry of private firms into an industry is often determined by government policy rather than by allowing industrial growth to take place by free entry and competition. In considerable measure, this pattern was promoted by an almost universally accepted conviction that economic growth depends upon rapid industrialization. This philosophy is strongly opposed by sustainable development economists, who advocate the allocation of more capital and technology to the rural areas.

Environmental problems in the urban/industrial areas of Third World countries are similar to those that existed in Western countries in the early part of the present century. Air pollution from household and industrial burning of high-sulfur coal; from heavy industries, such as cement, fertilizer, iron and steel, nonfuel mineral smelters, petroleum refineries and petrochemicals; from motor vehicles; and from power generating facilities that burn fossil fuels. For example, the daily maximum average sulfur dioxide and suspended particulate matter (SPM) in Ankara, Turkey during 1984–5 was seven to eight times the medically safe levels recommended by the World

Health Organization (WHO). Water pollution is acute in most metropolitan areas, where industries discharge metals, organic substances, nutrients, and toxic waste, and where households and commercial enterprises discharge untreated effluent and solid waste into municipal sewers or adjacent surface waters. In many cities, fewer than half the dwellings are connected to a sewer pipe, and most municipal pipes discharge directly into surface waters or open drains. High-density housing in coastline cities discharges waste into the sea, with a consequent fouling of public beaches and destruction of fisheries. Port cities are notorious for marine oil spillage, which destroys aquatic life, pollutes wetlands, and fouls beaches. Most municipal solid waste is disposed of in open dumps, where it is left uncovered and untreated. These practices lead to contamination of storm water that drains into surface and groundwater and create breeding grounds for flies, rodents, and scavengers that spread disease. Domestic animals browse through unfenced dumps in search of food. Factories dump hazardous materials (including slag, dust, and metals) into adjacent surface waters, thus contributing to marine pollution. Solid waste collection is slow, inefficient, or nonexistent. There is little recycling or composting. Rivers and canals running through cities are often swills and carry disease. The list goes on.

The reasons for the lack of control of pollution in Third World countries range from the absence of legislation, institutional arrangements or controls (as in the case of Ghana), to the absence of standards for regulation or of enforcement (as in the case of Turkey). The 'polluter pays' principle is well established in Turkish legislation, but few incentives exist for industrial firms to curb pollution. In Pakistan there is a multiplicity of legislation, at both the federal and provincial levels, governing all aspects of the environment and natural resource management. There exists an Environmental Protective Council (chaired by the President of Pakistan) and a Pakistan Environmental Protection Agency. There are also requirements for the submission of environmental impact assessments on proposed projects that might harm the environment. The machinery exists, but it does not operate. Controls on industrial waste emissions are virtually nonexistent and sewage and solid waste disposal facilities in many of the largest cities are less than half those required. A recent survey of the chemical industry found that only three of 100 plants treat waste in accordance with international standards.

Reasons for urban pollution in Third World countries

The abysmal environmental record of Third World countries is not due to a lack of knowledge about environmental degradation and its effects on human welfare and productivity. There are many people in and out of government who are quite aware of the problems. The fact that governments dominate industries in most Third World countries might appear to facilitate implementation of environmental protection, to which most governments at least pay lip service. But government ownership and operation is a major reason for the absence of environmental controls. One branch of the government finds it difficult or impossible to impose controls on other branches. State enterprises are often autonomous and beyond the control of the ministry responsible for the environment. Production has a higher priority than social welfare, and the fact that one industry's waste disposal reduces the productivity of other industries fails to generate a popular demand for controls. Until recently, most developing countries were dictatorships, or under the control of government bureaucracies and industrial and financial leaders unresponsive to social demands. There has been a general absence of grassroots movements demanding social reforms that affect the welfare of individuals, as contrasted with interests represented by labor union leaders, landowners, businessmen, and politicians. In many countries, environmental NGOs with political clout are almost unknown.

The close association between government and industry in developing countries would appear to facilitate enforcement of environmental regulations. Just the opposite is the case. Governments have great difficulty policing themselves. It is easier for an environmental authority to force a private firm to obey regulations than to force compliance by a large government enterprise whose head is often politically powerful. The government enterprise may argue that it lacks the funds to acquire equipment for reducing sulfur dioxide emissions or for changing its method of waste disposal. (The alternative of shutting down a large government enterprise is generally not politically possible.)

It is usually easier to develop an institutional framework to control private activities than to control government operations. This is true in the United States, where the Environmental Protection Agency (EPA) has had great difficulty controlling the environmental practices of the Department of Defense. It is sometimes easier for NGOs to obtain private entity compliance with environmental legislation through the courts than for them to sue the government directly. In the USA, political pressure from NGOs representing a variety of constituents plays a major role in enforcing environmental laws and regulations, as well as in bringing about new legislation. Such activities are the essence of a democratic society. Nondemocratic countries are unlikely to have a fully effective environmental program. It is also true that pressure on local government to build adequate sewage treatment facilities and to handle solid waste and hazardous materials in a manner that will protect community health will be more effective than decrees emanating from the federal government. Although federal laws might set minimum standards, perhaps enforced by the withholding of grants, stricter standards may require actions by local governments demanded by community NGOs.

Unfortunately, democracy at the community level does not exist in most Third World countries.

New Industrial Projects

The approach of the World Bank and other multilateral development banks (MDBs) to environmental protection has been to require environmental impact assessments (EIAs) for new projects as a condition of financial support. This procedure has also been adopted by governments for industrial projects, regardless of the source of financing. However, this approach will require decades before there can be a significant reduction in industrial pollution, and it will not assure that new plants continue to operate in accordance with their initial specifications. Therefore, industrial pollution should be dealt with by emissions standards applied to all sources of particular pollutants. In most countries what is required is a revamping of all environmental legislation, a restructuring of government at the ministerial level to give one ministry full control over all government actions affecting the environment, including the military, and the creation of a nonpolitical administrative structure free of influence by business, landowners, or other special interests. This may seem utopian in some countries where governments at almost all levels are fraudulent and serve special interests more than public welfare.

Eastern Europe

Environmental degradation of the industrial–urban centers of Eastern Europe is similar to that in many Third World countries except that it is on a larger scale. Air pollution is staggering, with sulfur dioxide levels in some cities five to ten times US standards. Much of the air pollution is caused by the burning of lignite or brown coal, which is high in sulfur. Energy is used inefficiently: the former Soviet Union and Eastern European countries consume 50–100 percent more energy per dollar of GDP than the USA and 100–300 percent more than Japan (French, 1990, p. 12). Industrial waste and untreated municipal sewage have been dumped into the rivers so that most are badly polluted. Many rivers and lakes in Eastern Germany are biologically dead and both surface and groundwater are contaminated by metals, organic waste, and nitrates.

These conditions were not the result of ignorance on the part of the communist governments – a substantial body of legislation exists. The standards were ignored by plant managers because their success was measured by quantity of output and not by contribution to social welfare. Studies of environmental conditions carried out by communist government agencies were suppressed, and private publications and public protests were illegal under the communist regimes. As is the case in Third World countries, government ownership and suppression of civil liberties were directly correlated with environmental degradation. In Czechoslovakia, East Germany and Poland, green parties were active and played an important role in the 1989 revolutions, and the new governments have made environmental reforms an important part of their agendas. On becoming Provisional President of Czechoslovakia, Vaclav Havel stated: 'We have laid waste to our soil and the rivers and the forests that our forefathers bequeathed to us, and we have the worst environment in the whole of Europe today' (French, 1990, p. 38). One of Havel's first actions was to appoint prominent environmentalists to prepare reports and proposals for new environmental laws.

The costs of cleaning up Eastern Europe are staggering, running to hundreds of billions of dollars, and many large plants have been or will need to be shut down with a consequent loss of output and employment. Competing requirements for the capital to rehabilitate the economies are so large that there is concern that environmental programs will be greatly delayed. The most rapid progress is likely to be made by Eastern Germany, since as a part of unified Germany it will be required to meet West German standards. One estimate of the cost of bringing Eastern Germany's environment up to standard is $249–$308 billion over a ten-year period (French, 1990, p. 40). External sources of capital, such as the World Bank and the new European Bank for Reconstruction and Development (EBRD), are required to attach stringent environmental conditions to their loans and projects. However, program loans and technical assistance are needed to institute environmental programs covering all industries and municipal waste disposal facilities.

The pace of environmental reform in Eastern Europe will be determined in large measure by the rate at which industry is privatized, and the rate of industrial rehabilitation and recapitalization. Foreign investment will also play a positive role since an effort will be made to require foreign firms to conform to Western standards and, in any case, new industrial projects will be required to meet Western standards. Progress in Czechoslovakia, Eastern Germany, and Poland is likely to be greater than in Bulgaria and Romania. The pace of transition to private enterprise market economies in the Commonwealth of Independent States (CIS) will be critical to environmental progress, and this will depend upon a number of political developments that are not yet clear.

Development Priorities and the Environment

In both Eastern European and Third World countries with important industrial sectors, environmental reform will necessarily change development priorities and capital allocation. Primary emphasis on industrial production, which has led to environmental crises in the urban–industrial areas, should be abandoned in favor of investment allocation based on maximization of net social benefits and the addition of environmental costs to production costs. Technologies and energy sources need to be changed and, in many cases, comparative advantage will be shifted so that some goods will no longer be produced. By requiring environmental costs to be internalized, some heavy industries may be abandoned. Thousands of plants in Eastern Europe are being shut down because the cost of conversion is too great. Only the most modern steel plants, nonfuel mineral smelters, and fertilizer plants can operate in an environmentally acceptable manner and still compete in world markets. This is likely to change patterns of world trade and investment in pollution-intensive industries. A combination of the shifting of state ownership to private enterprise operating in competitive world markets on the one hand, and internalization of environmental costs on the other, will inevitably lead to major shifts in world comparative advantage.

Irrigation Projects

Since the Second World War, Third World irrigation projects have probably absorbed more capital and affected more people than any other project category (Mikesell and Williams, 1992, Chapter 4). An estimated $250 billion has been spent on irrigation projects, much of it financed by external assistance. Irrigated agriculture has existed from prehistoric times and there are many types. Irrigated land represents about 20 percent of the total area under cultivation, but produces over half the agricultural output. Irrigation is reported to be responsible for much of the recent increase in agricultural output in developing countries, and an expansion of irrigation is believed to be necessary to meet food requirements for the growing population, and to reduce poverty.

The type of irrigation that is most important today consists of damming rivers and creating reservoirs from which water is drawn for agricultural fields. It is this type that has created the most serious environmental and resource problems. Frequently the dams serve to provide both hydroelectric power and irrigation, and in many cases power generation has dominated both dam design and operation. There is growing controversy over the net social benefits of large dams after taking into account the adverse environmental impacts. This issue is not about the desirability of irrigation, but concerns the type of system.

The indictment against irrigation dams is large and impressive, and there are numerous case studies illustrating environmental and resource harm. In addition to environmental harm, many dam projects can be shown to be uneconomic in the sense that the monetary costs of their construction and operation exceed the monetary benefits. In most cases social costs would be much higher than the monetary costs if allowance were made for the nonmonetary costs created by the dams and not included as costs incurred by the project. Some of the harmful environmental impacts are:

(1) *Water quality.* Water quality downstream from the dam is impaired by holding water in reservoirs, by diverting irrigation water from the river, and by the return flow from the irrigated fields. Impurities added to the water in dangerous concentration include toxic chemicals, organic matter causing a variety of diseases, nitrates, and phosphates that contribute to eutrophication, which causes waterweed proliferation.

(2) *Soil modification.* Irrigation waters may contain large amounts of salt, which concentrates in fields and limits crop production. Salt can be leached from the soil by sufficient water inputs from irrigation or rainfall, but highly saline water pumped into rivers creates problems for those using downstream water.

(3) *Health hazards.* Reservoirs associated with dams are breeding areas for disease-causing organisms. The most important diseases are malaria, schistosomiasis (or bilharzia), dysentery, hepatitis, yellow fever, and sleeping sickness. Interrupting the normal stream flow provides a breeding place for insects, snails, and other organisms that serve as hosts for bacteria and worms that invade humans. These hazards are also present in canals and drainage ditches associated with irrigation projects. Irrigation also interrupts normal flooding, which may have both negative and beneficial effects on the health of downstream areas.

(4) *Natural resource destruction.* The creation of reservoirs that may occupy hundreds of square miles destroys forests, wildlife, and productive agricultural land.

(5) *Fisheries.* Dams stop fish migration in the rivers and fish ladders when built are not always effective. A US example is the loss of wild salmon in the Columbia River and its tributaries. However, the reservoirs themselves can provide an important habitat for fish. For example, in the Saguling reservoir in Indonesia, the fisheries helped those resettled to restore or even surpass their previous income from river fish. Similar results have occurred elsewhere.

(6) *Socioeconomic impacts.* Perhaps the most serious charge against large dams is that they have required the involuntary resettlement of thousands of people from areas inundated by reservoirs. In most cases compensation for property has been inadequate and satisfactory arrangements have not been made for resettling the evacuees. Villages have been destroyed without creating new communities with appropriate infrastructure where evacuees have the opportunity to resettle.

Many of these harmful impacts can be prevented or greatly mitigated, but where this cannot be done compensatory measures can be taken, such as full compensation to those forced to resettle. However, some of the harm done by large irrigation dams arises from poor management of the irrigation system. Fees for water use are often based on the amount of land irrigated rather than on the amount of water actually used. This leads to overuse of water, which causes waterlogging of the soil and a consequent loss of productivity. Measures to protect downstream users of the river may not be taken, and frequently there is failure to take measures against health hazards created by the reservoir and irrigation systems. Government agencies responsible for construction and operation of irrigation projects often fail to internalize the social costs, such as the full cost of resettling evacuees. Promises made to the residents of the area when the project is proposed, as well as promises made to external financing agencies, are not kept.

A frequently noted criticism of large irrigation systems is that they subsidize well-to-do farmers who own or are able to obtain irrigated land, while creating economic hardship for others. Subsidies take the form of the provision of irrigated water or other services at less than cost and at the expense of those not fully compensated for damage done to their property, livelihood, and general well-being. All projects should be at least neutral in their effects on the distribution of income. It is a violation of the Pareto optimality rule if an increase in total social benefits is achieved at the expense of some members of society.[2]

A distributional problem may arise when the dam is also used for hydroelectric power. Power rates to urban users are often low and do not cover the full costs of power transmission and generation. Again, this involves a subsidy to people who are better off economically than those in the area of the dam, who bear the social cost of the enterprise. In some cases, even the direct costs attributed to power are not covered in the prices paid by those who benefit. Although these conditions are important problems in Third World development, there is abundant experience with them in developed countries, particularly in the western United States. Users of irrigation water in California pay only a fraction of the full social costs of dams and irrigation systems, and the power that brought aluminum and other energy-intensive industries to the Pacific Northwest is sold at rates that do not cover the damage to the river systems and the fishing industry – once a major source of livelihood and recreation for those living in the area.

Irrigation systems and development policy

Irrigation and water management specialists do not agree on the net social benefits of large dams. Some argue against any new large dams and favor terminating those in various stages of completion (Goldsmith and Hildyard, 1984, pp. 331–2). Others believe that, for large areas served by rivers, large reservoirs are more cost-effective than a number of small watershed developments (Crosson, 1987). Still others take a more cautious approach that does not condemn all large dams, but point to the unsatisfactory project performance of many of them and the need to adopt procedures that take full account of their social and environmental impacts before undertaking new projects (Dixon *et al.*, 1989).

Almost no one doubts the importance of irrigation for expanding agricultural output. A number of specialists have emphasized alternatives to large dams, such as small reservoirs created by diverting only a portion of a river, retaining water overflow in periods of heavy rainfall, and using groundwater for irrigation. Some argue that in the light of the rising cost of new dams, irrigation funds would be better spent by improving the existing surface systems, expanding groundwater extraction, and combining the use of groundwater with surface water irrigation (Svendsen and Meinzen-Dick, 1991, pp. 42–70). Clearly, there is a need for better project evaluation by both host governments and the MDBs supporting irrigation projects than has been carried out in the past. Some examples of project failures are given in the case studies presented in Chapter 6.

Irrigation projects provide good examples of the desirability of combining traditional development analysis with environmental and resource economics. Countries such as India and Pakistan have been devoting a high proportion of their available capital, including their ability to obtain foreign financing, to irrigation and hydropower. It is not sufficient to make decisions on proposed multipurpose dam projects on the basis of their realizing a minimum return on the capital investment. There are important opportunity costs for the use of both capital and natural resources that should be taken into account. Less costly projects leave capital available for other uses that may yield larger net social benefits, and alternative uses of natural resources may involve lower social costs in an intergenerational context. Applying environmental and sustainability criteria reveals the social costs often neglected in conventional project evaluation.

Other Agricultural and Land-Use Policies

Development planners in Third World countries in combination with the staffs of external assistance agencies have often transferred technologies and agricultural practices that have proved inappropriate for the local farming industry and/or are inconsistent with sustainable development. Many of these transfers are in line with traditional development strategy that fosters equipment and inputs similar to those found in developed economies. Economic growth has been associated with modernization of technology, with the development of domestic and foreign markets, and with rapid capital formation facilitated by access to commercial credits. Some innovations, such as freer markets and the substitution of price incentives for traditional practices and government intervention, have promoted output and productivity. But other innovations have not been successful from the standpoint of either short-term economic benefits or sustainability. In this section I review briefly some of the less successful innovations.

Mechanized farming

Mechanization of farming has played a key role in the agricultural miracles in the United States and other countries with similar soil, climate, and land–labor ratio. While mechanization has been responsible for considerable soil loss for many decades, the USA could afford this loss without lowering output. Mechanization has also been successful in Asia when used only for specific tasks and following many generations of animal-drawn plowing. However, mechanized tilling has been used with disastrous results in the Brazilian Amazon following clearance of the forests, and has been a failure in several sub-Saharan countries in areas where animal traction had not been established beforehand.

Following independence, several African governments promoted crop-cultivation schemes under which groups of farms were managed and operated as a single unit or with tractor hire arrangements for multifarm use of equipment. But the mechanization schemes (some supported by MDB loans) adopted by Zimbabwe, Kenya, Zambia, Malawi, Tanzania, and the Ivory Coast, among others, turned out to be fiascos. Unlike countries in Asia, these countries had little experience with animal-drawn plowing on which to build tractor tillage. These programs were started in the mid-1960s, but by the mid-1980s few tractors remained in operation. Where they were still in use, they were usually associated with rice cultivation and privately owned. In many cases soil conditions led to erosion following mechanization and were not suitable for the crops that were grown. Moreover, capital costs were very high in relation to labor costs, and there was difficulty in obtaining spare parts, which had to be bought with foreign exchange. During the 1980s, government emphasis shifted to encouraging the use of improved hand tools and animal-drawn equipment (Pingali *et al.*, 1987, Chapter 6).

Chemical pesticides and fertilizers

The decline of traditional farming methods in developing countries, including crop rotation, fallow, and the use of animal manures, led to a rapid loss of nutrients in the soil and increased vulnerability to pests. This led to a chemical revolution in farming in many Third World countries, often promoted by billions of dollars worth of pesticides and fertilizers supplied by MDBs and bilateral foreign assistance agencies, either directly through agricultural development loans or indirectly through support of agricultural credit programs. These programs encouraged governments to subsidize the sale of the commodities to local farmers who came to depend heavily upon them. As was discovered in the USA, toxic pesticides are human health hazards, while chemical fertilizers contribute to pollution of waterways and wetlands. In many countries, subsidized commodities have led to overuse, and heavy dependence has resulted in disasters in periods when foreign exchange shortage or the absence of foreign aid rendered the commodities unavailable. Also, using pesticides may prove self-defeating since insects develop a resistance to them.

Efforts should be made by foreign assistance agencies to shift Third World farmers from heavy dependence on chemical pesticides and fertilizers. Organic farming and the use of biological control techniques and resistant varieties of seed for dealing with pests represent modern trends in Western countries, which should be adopted by developing countries in the interest of preserving their soil. In many cases this will require research and experimentation to determine the most cost-effective methods consistent with agricultural sustainability.

Subsidized agricultural credits

Treatises on Third World agriculture frequently point to the lack of availability of agricultural credits on reasonable terms to finance capital expenditures and shifts from subsistence farming to more profitable production for domestic and foreign markets. Many farmers must rely on local moneylenders, who charge exorbitant interest rates and require short loan maturities. Encouraged by foreign assistance agencies, most governments in developing countries maintain agricultural credit programs. Agricultural credit loans have been very popular with MDBs. For example, the World Bank and IDA alone made nearly $10 billion in agricultural credit loans from the beginning of operations to 30 June 1990 (World Bank, 1990a, p. 177).

Although the creation of efficient capital markets in rural areas of developing countries would undoubtedly promote investment and increased productivity, agricultural economists have recently been critical of government-sponsored subsidized credits to farmers. They point out that regulated low-interest loans discourage private financial institutions from serving rural markets and impair their ability to mobilize rural savings, since rural savers tend to channel their savings to the metropolitan centers where they can earn a higher return. Moreover, subsidized credits may generate an excess demand for credit, which is often used for nonproductive purposes. Because subsidized credits must be rationed, government credit agencies tend to favor wealthy farmers or those with political connections (Krueger *et al.*, 1989, pp. 162-7). A better approach is to provide technical assistance and loans at market rates of interest to private regional financial institutions that will encourage rural savings and provide credits to farmers at rates that cover administrative costs. In many cases, these institutions are best owned and operated by locally managed farm cooperatives or by nonprofit NGOs.

Modernization versus traditional agriculture

In the literature on agriculture in poor countries, there is a debate among specialists over modernization versus a return to traditional practices. This issue is especially critical in sub-Saharan Africa, where rapid population growth and improper agricultural practices are destroying the soil and promoting desertification. The traditional methods of rotating crops, fallowing, animal manure, small-scale irrigation, and primitive tilling preserved the soil for centuries. This suggests that traditional methods involving less intensive farming and less chemical and mechanical inputs should be recommended for sustainability. But traditional farming methods that succeeded in periods of virtually stationary population and with large amounts of undeveloped land cannot meet the food requirements of a rapidly growing population with virtually no frontier land. Expanding the food supply without continued depletion of the soil requires greater farming intensity of arable land, more productive seeds and other material inputs, proper product selection from the standpoint of productivity and markets, and scientific tilling, planting, and water control methods based on research and pilot projects oriented to conditions in particular areas. Such a program is neither traditional nor based on the borrowing of the state-of-the-art methods from the West. It must also recognize social and institutional conditions, including the pattern of farm ownership and tenancy, the existence of common grazing areas, and the role of tribal chiefs and village organizations in controlling land use.

In line with conventional agricultural development doctrine, MDB assistance has supported extensive agriculture, including the opening of frontier areas, infrastructure (including major roads, but not feeder roads), large irrigation projects, cattle ranching, and plantation development. None of these approaches has provided a solution to the twin problems of expanding food supply and halting soil degradation. A group of penetrating and frank studies by World Bank agricultural specialists covering six sub-Saharan African countries concluded that the external donors that have poured billions of dollars into these six countries made little contribution to their agricultural output.[3] The summary study (Lele, 1989, p. 41) acknowledges the 'relatively small role that donor assistance has played in the growth that has occurred in MADIA countries. Large amounts of aid have been allocated with the best of intentions, to types of activities that have had little effect on growth.' These findings are supported by reports of other specialists (Barnes and Olivares, 1988; Davis and Schirmer, 1987; Repetto, 1988; World Bank, 1989).

The authors of the African studies referred to above advocate donor support for broadly based sustainable agricultural programs that include the following elements: (a) balancing food and export crops; (b) greater use of African institutional and human capacity; (c) human capital and institutional development; (d) soil management and integration of cropping with livestock and forestry; and (e) research tailored to the needs of small farmers. All of this would require a longer-term perspective – 15 to 20 years – for sequencing an agricultural development strategy for a given country (Lele and Meyers, 1989, pp. 59–60).

There does not exist a detailed blueprint that will insure sustainable agricultural development in all Third World countries. Short-term remedies, such as providing credits, promoting agricultural exports, capital infusion in the form of infrastructure and large irrigation projects, and the development of frontier areas – all frequently found in development textbooks – have not been successful in promoting sustainable development. Each area requires research, experimentation, and pilot projects to determine what will succeed over time.

Parklands and Wildlife

A final topic that is given prominence and detailed attention in books on sustainable development, but is largely ignored in conventional development texts, is parklands and wildlife. Most developing countries have vast areas, often covering thousands of square miles, of tropical forests and other marginal lands in mountains and desert regions that can be set aside as preserves without disturbing the economic activities of inhabitants. Many of these areas still contain large numbers of wildlife, wetlands, scenic rivers, important watersheds that are the source of the country's major rivers, and unique biological diversity. Traditional development treatises generally overlook the long-run value of these ecosystems and their contributions to the productivity of the occupied sectors of the country. In some cases, their more immediate value as sources of tourist income is recognized, but rarely discussed is their economic and potential amenity value for the domestic population. Parks, forest reserves, and wildlife refuges provide sufficiently large social and economic benefits to justify their being given a high priority in development programs consistent with sustainability.

MDBs are beginning to require wildlife preservation as a condition for large projects that have an adverse effect on wildlife. The specific conditions sometimes include the maintenance of wildlife corridors between forested areas separated by reservoirs, dams, and highways, or the establishment of wildlife reserves to take the place of habitat destroyed by development. Thus, the external damage to wildlife is becoming internalized as a part of the projects supported by external assistance agencies.

Livestock Projects

Keeping herds of domesticated animals predates agriculture and permanent settlements, and remains an important occupation in Third World countries. More recently, large-scale commercial ranching has come to dominate the livestock industry in many countries and such projects are often financed by governments with support from MDBs. They can be a major source of environmental damage, especially when ranches are developed from tropical rainforests, from upland areas with fragile soils, or from areas traversed by large wildlife migrations. Although cattle grazing can be an important source of export earnings and domestic food, it may divert land and water from crop production, which usually produces higher net social benefits. This is basically a question of misallocation of land, but it can have environmental consequences if land shortage contributes to the overuse of marginal lands and excessive deforestation by peasants seeking land to grow food. Where livestock ranchers fail to maintain the pasture by overgrazing, or allow pesticide runoff into streams and lakes, they contribute directly to environmental degradation. Where they impede wildlife migration with fences or their herds compete with wildlife for grazing, there is wildlife destruction. Since cattle ranches usually do not combine crop raising with cattle grazing, manure is not used as crop fertilizer. Manure fertilizer contributes to the preservation of the soil. These factors need to be taken into consideration by governments in their policies and programs affecting land use allocation.

Overgrazing is frequently attributed to the use of a common pasture by a number of herders. Each herder has an interest in preserving or improving the common pasture, but unless action is taken collectively the individual herder does not benefit significantly, and actually incurs a net loss if he alone elects to limit his herd or invest labor and capital in the common pasture. This condition, which may lead to a steady deterioration of pasturelands, is sometimes spoken of as 'the tragedy of the commons.'

One remedy for this 'tragedy' is for the government to divide the common pasture into private fields or ranches and encourage each herder to fence his land. In the early 1970s the government of Botswana initiated a program that provided, among other things, for the creation of fenced ranches as a partial replacement of the commons system, which the government believed was encouraging overstocking. The program was financed in part by a World Bank loan in 1972, followed by additional loans in 1977 and 1985. The provisions of these loans supporting the creation of commercial ranches have been quite controversial, both within Botswana and in conservation organizations in the USA and Western Europe. A major criticism of the government program was that the ranches were established in areas in northern Botswana where there are regular migrations of wildlife. Thousands of wildebeest and other wild animals were killed trying to cross the fences. Also, it was argued that only well-to-do Botswanans could afford to fence and provide water and other facilities for their own ranches, leaving the poor herders to compete in the commons. Moreover, some of those owning ranches allowed their surplus cattle to graze in the commons. It was argued that if technical and financial support were given to communities and associations of herders using common pasture, they would develop rules on stocking and joint programs for maintaining the pastures. It has been pointed out that such arrangements have existed in some areas for hundreds of years. Livestock specialists remain divided on this issue.

Exporting Natural Resources

Traditional development textbooks gave special emphasis to the production and export of raw materials as a means of promoting economic growth. Selling the products of forests, mines, and plantations generates foreign exchange income needed to support capital investment in industry and agriculture. A number of export-induced growth models were formulated in which income from exports had a multiplier effect on domestic income, which in turn stimulated domestic production and investment. Much of the capital for financing investment in the resource-export industries came from developed countries, and the foreign investors brought technology and capital for promoting both the export industries and production for the domestic market.

This prescription for growth was strongly rejected by economists and politicians in developing countries during the early post-Second World War period, but often for the wrong reasons. Dependence on resource exports was regarded as a form of exploitation of poor countries by developed countries, and was seen as making the raw material exporters vulnerable to both cyclical price fluctuations and an alleged long-term decline in the terms of trade (i.e. prices of raw materials tend to decline relative to prices of manufactured imports). Developing countries were urged to promote substitutes for imports by channeling capital into domestic manufactures. This was accomplished by high protection on imports of manufactures, which reduced the internal terms of trade of their own raw material producers, thereby discouraging investment in resource industries. This practice was strongly criticized by mainstream development economists because it led to inefficient domestic production, lower investment and productivity in agriculture for the domestic market, and reduced foreign exchange income for buying essential imports and servicing foreign debt. The alleged long-run decline in terms of trade for raw materials was rightly regarded as a myth.

We have now come full circle. Environmental economists as well as environmentalists generally are urging developing countries to conserve their forests, to discourage mining when their construction and operation does environmental harm, and to avoid certain types of plantations that damage the soil. It has also been noted that the classic formula for growth through resource exports has not worked for most developing countries. The pattern of development followed by the USA, Canada, Australia, and New Zealand has not been duplicated by the developing countries during the second half of the twentieth century. The reasons for this are complex, but the lesson is not that natural resource exports impede growth, but that they are not sufficient for sustainable development.

The countries experiencing the highest growth rates since the Second World War (e.g. Japan, Korea, and Taiwan) did not have large natural resource exports, but increased their exports of manufactures. The way these countries achieved rapid growth was mainly by borrowing and importing Western technology, and by learning to operate very efficiently. Again, contrary to traditional economic doctrine, rapid growth cannot be attributed to massive doses of external capital, but is largely accounted for by increases in productivity (Solow, 1957). Thus, the modern prescription for growth is to give high priority to investment in education, training, and social capital, including health care and decent housing, and to provide an economic structure that rewards work and saving and provides freedom to innovate and experiment. This is consistent with sustainable development, which tends to be critical of natural resource exports that create environmental damage.

Forest Management

The strongest criticism of Third World environmental practices by the international conservation community is directed at the wanton destruction of tropical rainforests. This position is shared by a small but growing number of people in Third World countries. Some of the depletion of tropical forests has arisen from the rapid expansion of logging since the Second World War, mainly for export. But much of it has occurred as a result of converting forest lands to agriculture and cattle ranching. As population has grown and cultivatable land has become scarce, migrants have entered the frontier areas to acquire land. This process has been promoted by governments through road construction into rainforest areas, and in some cases by subsidized credits and the granting of titles to the forest lands. These countries are doing just what the settlers did in the American West during the nineteenth century.

Forests, once covering about half the land in tropical countries, have been disappearing rapidly and, if present trends continue, half or more of the remaining tropical forests will be gone by the year 2000. Before the Second World War, the largest forest losses occurred in the temperate forests of the industrialized countries; the tropical rainforests were until recently largely inaccessible and sparsely populated. Deforestation in the Third World is occurring at an estimated rate of 11 million hectares (ha) per year and is accelerating (Repetto and Gillis, 1988; Hertel and Hertel, 1989). For some countries, a continuation of current depletion rates will result in the elimination of forests by the end of this century, while for other countries, such as Brazil, total depletion is not imminent. But the loss of large portions of the tropical forests will have serious regional and global environmental impacts.

Forests are important for maintaining soil quality, limiting erosion, stabilizing hillsides, modulating seasonal flooding, and protecting watersheds and the watercourses that flow from them. Thus they contribute to agricultural productivity and to the many services that water provides. They are the major reservoir for biodiversity and millions of species are found only in tropical forests. Finally, they have an important impact on the atmosphere, both regional and global. They affect regional rainfall, and their absorption of carbon dioxide (and emission of carbon dioxide when they are burned) affects the accumulation of greenhouse gases. It is for this reason that tropical forests are of the greatest interest to people in the developed world. There is also great concern with the preservation of species (many of which are not yet identified), which would inevitably become extinct with the disappearance of the tropical forests.

Development policy and tropical deforestation

Tropical forests differ from temperate zone forests in several respects. First, sustained yields of commercially valuable trees may not be possible in tropical forests, except for selective logging of particular species. Second, the land is often not productive for agriculture after the trees are logged. Third, large tropical forests are often a source of important nontimber products, such as animals for food, latex, nuts, fruits and medicinal plants, and may provide a livelihood for indigenous people. These conditions complicate determination of which use of forest areas would provide the largest net social benefits. There is also uncertainty regarding the best use of tropical areas after they have been deforested; in some regions it has been possible to use land for crops on a continuous basis, but not in others. There is a need for more research and pilot studies.

Optimal development does not require the preservation of all tropical forests. To take an extreme case, a country that is 90 percent forested and has a growing population should not be advised to refrain from expanding its land area for agriculture and other uses. However, in clearing forests for other economic uses, governments should make sure the forest products are utilized and not simply destroyed by burning, and that the social benefits from alternative uses well exceed the opportunity costs of leaving the forest in its natural state. This latter principle has been violated in the Brazilian

Amazon and in other rainforest areas. For example, areas have been burned with no attempt to save the valuable lumber, while the logged areas have not been productive for crops for more than a few years, following which the land is left to erode. In the process, the livelihood of indigenous people who hunt animals and gather latex and other forest products has been destroyed. In some cases the major purpose of the government has been to meet a political demand for land rather than to maximize the net social product.

One argument for destroying tropical forests to provide agricultural land is that workers who are without land or without employment are producing nothing, and even if they engage in slash and burn agriculture they will be producing something. Maximizing employment as a social goal is not the same as maximizing the net social product. Although it is important for unemployed workers to find work, if the method of employment destroys resources that have productive value now or in the future, the result may be a negative net social product. It may be more economical for the surplus labor to be used to farm existing cultivatable land more intensively, or to be used in industry, say, for producing goods for export. To achieve such an adjustment it may be necessary to allow market forces to adjust prices of both labor and products, or for the government to provide tax or other incentives to promote the adjustment.

In the management of tropical forests, a distinction should be made among several types of violation of sustainable development principles. There is the destruction of the forest by burning, cutting, and bulldozing to clear the area without economic use being made of the timber or other products. This usually occurs because there are no facilities for hauling or processing logs in the area. Had there been a government plan for forest clearing before settlement, valuable timber could have been saved. In addition, clearance of land for agricultural use can take place while substantial stands of timber are left to protect the watershed, the streams, and the wildlife. Agro-forestry, in which crops and trees grow together, is another alternative. It is also important to determine in advance what agricultural uses are economical on cleared tropical forestland, since it may not sustain certain crops. Whether any agricultural use of the land is warranted as an alternative to maintaining the forest ecosystem must be determined. However, it is possible to choose a path that retains some of the advantages of sparing the forest.

Much of the loss of social benefits from tropical forests comes from the way in which they are managed for timber production. Government failure to protect forests may result in the use of timber for fuelwood, which yields a much lower value than commercial lumber. Economic timber management requires maximization of the present value of the tree harvest revenues. This means that harvest must take place at the proper time and that the timber is not wasted. However, economic management is not the same as sustainable forest management, which requires the maintenance of revenues over time and the avoidance of ecological damage. Most tropical forests are not economically managed and probably none is sustainably managed. A common government practice is to negotiate contracts with private firms to exploit the timber over a period of 20 years or so. The private contractors seek to maximize their revenues by removing the most valuable trees, take no interest in future harvests, and have no interest in protecting the forest ecology. Governments may also be more interested in immediate revenue than in sustained timber production.

Sustainable forestry

There is some question as to whether sustainable forestry is possible on an economic basis in tropical moist forests. All commercial forestry that requires road-building and the introduction of heavy equipment is incompatible with the sustainability of the forest ecosystem. Whether wood can be harvested from tropical moist forests on a sustainable basis is not clear. For 150 years teak forests in Burma were selectively extracted for use by the British Navy, but the trees were cut by hand and transported by elephants and riverboats – methods that are relatively nondamaging. Also, harvesting was done on 30-year rotations. Such methods may not be economic today. A study by World Bank economists (Goodland et al., 1990, p. 28) concludes that sustainable forestry in tropical moist forests is only possible on a low-yield basis with long rotations and very selective extractions. This study recommends that where forests are rapidly disappearing (e.g. Ivory Coast, Nigeria, Ghana, Papua New Guinea), the remaining primary forests should be protected and logging limited to secondary forests and plantations. Some students of tropical forests have recommended the utilization of forest products, such as oil, nuts, medicines, and animals for meat, without commercial logging, thus preserving the biodiversity and the way of life of native dwellers. There are also various types of agro-forestry that maintain tree cover and preserve part of the forest ecology. There is need for considerable experimentation on the uses of tropical forests that might provide net social benefits equivalent to commercial logging, and that would sustain the forest ecosystem. There is also an important social value in retaining tropical forests for the global value of limiting the accumulation of greenhouse gases that affect world climate.

Global forests and global benefits

It is believed that world forests absorb a significant amount of carbon dioxide and therefore tend to offset some of the emissions that cause global warming. When forests are destroyed by fire, there is a net addition to carbon dioxide emissions. Because a large proportion of the world's remaining forests are in Third World countries, developed countries have shown a special interest in preserving them for their own benefit. There is also a world interest in preserving the plant and animal species in tropical forests. It is difficult to measure the social benefits of preventing the extinction of species and of maintaining unique ecosystems. For some people there is value in just knowing a rainforest is there, whether or not they ever intend to visit the Amazon basin or the tropical forests of Papua New Guinea. Millions of people will feel they have lost something when they learn that the last Brazilian jaguar or bearded Saki monkey has died. It might be possible to measure the value of the medical discoveries made over the past few decades in research on plants found in tropical forests, often with the aid of shamans belonging to indigenous tribes. Despite the great uncertainties regarding these global social values associated with maintaining the remaining tropical forest ecosystems, the global value of preserving them is undoubtedly greater than the global benefits from development. But this may not be true from a national perspective.

Recognition of global values in tropical forests and in other natural settings, such as wetlands used by transcontinental birds and marine breeding areas for aquatic life, has added a new dimension to sustainable development. Even where the individual nations do not attach much value to these natural resources yielding global benefits, other nations individually and collectively can increase their net social benefits by subsidizing the protection of these global resources. Both private organizations and governments are beginning to make monetary contributions (including forgiveness of debt) to Third World countries for the preservation of tropical forests and this practice could be extended to other natural resources that yield global returns. The value of these efforts becomes much greater when we consider the value to future generations of preserving the quality of the atmosphere and the genetic pool that has taken hundreds of million of years to create.

Land Resettlement

Much of the destruction of tropical forests has accompanied large resettlement programs undertaken by governments. These programs are usually designed to provide land ownership and occupation by landless peasants in frontier areas that are forested or were otherwise inaccessible in the past, or are marginal in productive quality. In most cases these lands would have already been occupied if they were of good quality for crops or readily accessible. In a few cases, inaccessibility of the area has been due to its location on outer islands that lack infrastructure. The land to be occupied is usually owned by the government or may be claimed (without legal title) by indigenous tribal people. In some cases, resettlement programs in Latin America have been undertaken as land reform programs in which large landholdings used for cattle grazing or simply as hunting reserves have been confiscated for distribution to small farmers. In such cases environmental harm can be done if improper methods of farming are used on marginal lands.

Large resettlements may be divided into three types: (a) government planned and sponsored programs for moving people (usually on a voluntary basis) to new areas; (b) voluntary, unplanned resettlement facilitated by new roads or railroads and/or induced by temporary job opportunities; and (c) involuntary resettlement arising from the creation of reservoirs. Probably the best known of the planned resettlements is the Indonesia Transmigration Program (ITMP), involving resettlement of more than two million people from the densely populated areas of Java and Bali to the outer islands of Sumatra, Kalimantan, Sulawesi, and Irian Jaya (see Chapter 6).

Unplanned migration has occurred all over the world in recent years, mainly to tropical forest areas or to upland areas where the soil is poor and vulnerable to erosion. Migration into the Brazilian Amazon has been both planned and unplanned, and frequently a combination of both. For example, the Polonoroeste Project in Rondonia in northwestern Brazil, initiated in 1982, was a land distribution program facilitated by construction of a new road from Brasilia into the Amazon area (see Chapter 6). Of the 700,000 migrants, only a fraction received lots from the federal land agency; most simply occupied and cleared land available for settlement and titling. Some settlers received credits, but there was little planning to provide the conditions for agricultural success or to prevent the wanton destruction of the forests and general misuse of the land. In the involuntary migrations associated with irrigation projects, lack of planning often results in the evacuees settling in forests or upland areas where they do substantial environmental damage. In each of these types of migrations there are important cases where the rights of indigenous tribal people were violated and their cultures and means of livelihood harmed or destroyed.

Even though the unplanned nineteenth-century migrations to the western United States succeeded in creating prosperous farming communities (along with considerable environmental damage and violations of the rights of Native Americans), they do not provide a desirable model for Third World countries. The economic fruits of *laissez faire* do not arise from a grab-bag of public lands, and the environmental and social costs of spontaneous frontier communities are too high. Free enterprise works best under rules common to all participants – rules that safeguard the environment and avoid discrimination and subsidies that cannot be justified in terms of net social benefits. If public lands are to be made available for private ownership and the formation of new economic communities, a good deal of planning is called for to make the new communities viable, both economically and environmentally. Natural resources should be used on a sustainable basis and the government should capture some of the rents from public lands transferred in the form of land sales or rental payments. The government needs these rents to provide infrastructure for the new communities and to administer the migration program. In land distribution programs, governments should prevent acquisition of land by speculators as contrasted with productive farmers. Speculators, who are usually absentee owners, skim off the rents and raise the price of land, thereby increasing costs to operators. By paying more for land, operators have less capital to put into their productive activities, while the rents accruing to the speculators provide no social benefits.

In addition to resource protection and meeting the social needs for education, health and housing, planners of resettlement programs should be concerned with how new communities are integrated with the economy from which the migrants came. Failure to provide for exports from the new community and to enable trade in goods and services to take place with the source community may leave the new community without a means of self-support. Economic failure and poverty usually lead to natural resource destruction.

The above observations on new settlements are derived from the experience of migrations to frontier lands the world over. They question some of the advantages of opening frontier land found in traditional economic history and development books. The costs to the participants of spontaneous unplanned migrations have been shown to be great, but the long-run social costs of the natural resource destruction can be enormous to both present and future generations. This is another example of the perspective brought by sustainable development economics to traditional development doctrine.

Power

Investment in power generation and transmission is a major item in the capital budgets of developing countries and represents about 20 percent of total lending by MDBs. About half of the outlays for power generation has been for hydroelectric power and most of the remainder has been for thermal (oil, gas and coal). Traditional development policy has regarded investment in low-cost power as a precondition for industrialization and growth, and the lowest-cost power is usually hydroelectric, which can often be generated jointly with irrigation. However, hydropower generation and transmission may engender environmental and other social costs that are often overlooked by both governments and external assistance agencies. Power generation has often dominated the design of multipurpose dams at the expense of irrigation and, in most cases, the irrigation objective could be achieved at a much smaller cost and environmental disturbance without the power element. Also, power is often transmitted through hundreds of miles of tropical forest. This damages the forest and facilitates the intrusion of people seeking to exploit forest resources.

But do not the benefits from industrialization outweigh by many times the social cost of environmental damage created by hydropower? There is considerable evidence that this is not the case and that the advantages of low-cost hydropower are overstated. In most manufacturing industries, power is no more than 5 percent of total production cost, and the cost of power generation hundreds of miles from where it is consumed may represent only one-third of the total power cost. The availability of low-cost power will not in itself attract industry since there are many other conditions, such as the availability of raw materials at world market prices, government investment policies, wage rates and labor union practices, and the availability of markets, that are more important. Very often the demand for low-cost power is driven by urban consumers and the suppliers of electric appliances. In addition, most power supplied from publicly owned facilities in developing countries is priced below both monetary and social costs, so that urban dwellers are subsidized at the expense of the rural population. Because power generating and transmitting facilities constitute a large portion of the capital budgets of developing countries and have been responsible for a significant amount of their external debt, sustainable development policy requires that consideration be given to the opportunity costs of additional investment in power. Projected demand for power by industry and urban consumers in countries such as Brazil and India indicates that the demand for energy capacity will double over the next decade or so. But considering the need to limit external debt growth, and the capital and foreign exchange needs of other economic sectors, power generation may absorb too much of the available capital. Moreover, energy specialists have suggested that many developing countries could cut their need for increased power generating capacity by investing in more energy-efficient industrial equipment, lighting systems, air conditioning, and other electrical appliances at an investment cost of one-third that required to produce an equivalent amount of new power from generating facilities (Rich, 1990, p. 11). In poor countries, such as India and Pakistan and the countries of sub-Saharan Africa, so much investment is required to reduce abject poverty and assure even a modest growth in average per capita food consumption over the next several decades that these countries cannot afford a high rate of growth in power-intensive consumption, which benefits only a small percentage of the population.

This is not simply an equity issue in the allocation of capital, but involves the Pareto optimality principle of maximizing the social product without harming the welfare of any particular group. Setting prices for power that cover its full social costs, including environmental and resource depletion costs, would probably go a long way in dealing with the problem. This is another example of how sustainable development economics approaches a problem by applying *fully* the economic principles of internalizing external costs and of Pareto optimality.

Mining Projects

There are a number of developing countries whose major export industry is mining, much of the investment for which is provided by foreign capital in the form of equity or loans. For many countries mining has been the basis of their development, and expanding the mining sector is the best opportunity for growth. Yet mining and associated mineral processing is one of the most environmentally harmful activities and, until recently, little attention was paid to the environmental impacts of the industry. These impacts include soil destruction, sedimentation in rivers and lakes, toxic chemicals discharged into surface and groundwater, deforestation, the creation of large scars on the land, and air pollution from smelters. Most of the world's mines are located in mountainous areas far from population centers directly affected by pollution. In some countries only 'primitive' indigenous people are affected and they have not had sufficient political influence to obtain protection against the incursions of the mining industry. However, developing country governments can no longer ignore the environmental costs of mining projects. Democratically elected legislators have passed laws requiring air and water pollution abatement and the restoration of open-pit mine and mine tailing areas to agricultural production. There has also been international pressure on countries to protect the rights of indigenous people.

There are ways to design mining projects so that environmental damage can be kept to an acceptable level. Tailings and other waste can be kept out of rivers and lakes with dams, chemicals can be neutralized so that they will not pollute groundwater, and processing methods can be used that avoid emissions of sulfur dioxide and other atmosphere polluting gases. Chemicals used in processing ores are highly toxic (e.g. cyanide in gold extraction) and rainwater passing through tailings may become quite acidic. Mining firms can be required to put up bonds to guarantee they will clean up the mining area, including filling in an open pit at the termination of the operation. Also, comprehensive surveys are necessary to determine the geologic stability of the mining area and its vulnerability to earthquakes and volcanic activities, and to slides generated by heavy rainfall. All of these potential environmental hazards need to be identified in the EIA and the necessary measures for dealing with them should be embodied in the project design and feasibility study.

Difficulties may arise in carrying out these conditions, however. First, the EIA and the environmental safeguards are often very expensive, running to many millions of dollars. These outlays could run to as much as 20 percent of the capital cost of the mine. Unless the ores are very rich and other mining and transportation costs relatively low, the economic feasibility study might show that the mine could not be profitable. However, this would not be known before a costly EIA was undertaken. The full costs of environmental safeguards might not be known until they were actually undertaken because some costs are difficult to anticipate. As illustrated in the case study in Chapter 6 of the Ok Tedi copper and gold mining project in Papua New Guinea, this presents an especially difficult problem when mines are developed by foreign private investors. The final contract for the development of an ore body is often not negotiated until there has been an EIA and a feasibility study has been completed. Private mining companies are usually unwilling to make large expenditures until they have a final contract to develop and operate the mine and they are also unwilling to commit themselves to unlimited expenditures for environmental safeguards. Sometimes governments may be faced with a decision of whether to halt mining operations when the necessary measures to protect the environment are not taken by the mining company, or to allow the company to continue operating the mine. Faced with this decision on the Ok Tedi mine, the government of Papua New Guinea decided to allow the mining company to continue in violation of the government's environmental standards. Fortunately, most mining projects do not present the environmental problems associated with the Ok Tedi mine.

Mining also disturbs the economic and cultural life of tribal peoples in tropical forests, not simply by polluting their lands and rivers, but also by employing their people in the mines. There are a number of examples of indigenous tribes being adversely affected by gold and iron ore mining in the Amazon forest. The large copper mine established on the island of Bougainville was so resented by the local population that they staged a revolution, declaring independence from Papua New Guinea, and forced the multi-million dollar mine to close.

In cases where the government or private owner of a potential mining venture is unwilling or unable to undertake a full EIA for the project or where the cost of preventing severe environmental damage is so large that if undertaken the mine would be unlikely to be sufficiently profitable for the investment to be made, it would be better for the government not to allow the mine to be built. This may represent a hard decision for a government when the mine promises to yield millions of dollars in revenue, but if the social costs are properly estimated, with an allowance for risk of underestimation, the social costs may exceed the social gains.

Petroleum

Oil is where you find it, and it is often found in environmentally sensitive areas, such as tropical forests, parks and wildlife refuges, wetlands, delicate

Arctic environments, and in offshore areas rich in aquatic life. Public relations officials of petroleum companies sometimes circulate pictures of wildlife contentedly grazing near oil wells surrounded by tropical trees, or of caribou calmly crossing the tundra beneath suspended oil pipelines. What they don't say is that drilling wells and transporting oil by land or sea can be very damaging to the environment. Heavy equipment must be transported through forests to drill exploratory wells, and pipelines built across hundreds of miles of primary forest and wetlands if oil is found and produced. In addition, the construction of roads into frontier areas invites migrants to seek employment in petroleum communities or to exploit the forest resources. Migrants may come into conflict with indigenous people and contest their traditional rights to the land.

In 1990 an American oil company consortium led by Conoco negotiated an agreement with the Ecuadorian government to drill for oil in a region located in the Huaoroni Indigenous Reserve and in Yasuni National Park (*New York Times*, 1991, p. B8). The government and Conoco officials have sought to allay environmentalists' criticisms by taking measures to limit deforestation, patrol the 90-mile access road into the jungle to prevent an influx of settlers, bury the pipeline to reduce the cleared right of way, and protect the health and way of life of the Huaoroni Indians. Conoco officials also offered institutions, such as the New York Botannical Gardens and the Smithsonian Institution, the right to use the oil camps as outposts for research of the rainforest. These actions have not satisfied conservation groups, who steadfastly oppose petroleum operations in national parks, indigenous Indian reservations, and all areas with delicate environments. Nevertheless, the Ecuadorian case shows a strong interest on the part of international petroleum companies to reduce environmental damage caused by their operations. This interest has been encouraged by conservation organizations.

Summary

The foregoing analysis of the environmental and resource problems associated with major categories of projects and programs illustrates the need for environmental assessments by governments and external finance agencies. Such assessments go well beyond the conventional project evaluation undertaken before projects and programs are approved. However, sustainable development involves more than individual projects. There must be a comprehensive set of development policies for selecting the right projects for government support and for providing the private sector with the proper incentives for moving the entire economy along the path of sustainable development. These policies are examined in the next chapter.

NOTES

1 In traditional social benefit–cost analysis both benefits and costs are discounted so that benefits accruing 20 years or more in the future will have a relatively small value when compared with current benefits. Likewise, costs that will be borne well into the future are also heavily discounted. This practice applied to the use of natural resources tends to bias economic decisions against the welfare of future generations. The approach to project evaluation presented in Chapter 2, in which natural resource depletion and environmental degradation are treated as social costs, will avoid this bias.
2 Pareto optimality requires that economic resources be allocated in a manner that maximizes the net social product without reducing the real incomes of any individuals or group. Where maximizing the net social product has the effect of reducing the income of an individual or group, gainers from the increase in the social product should compensate the losers.
3 The donor agencies are: World Bank, USAID, UK Overseas Development Administration, Swedish International Development Authority, Danish International Development Agency, the European Community, and the governments of France and West Germany.

REFERENCES

Barnes, Douglas F. and Olivares, Jose (1988) *Sustainable Resource Management in Agriculture and Rural Development Projects: A Review of Bank Policies, Procedures, and Results*, Environment Department Working Paper no. 5. Washington, DC: World Bank.

Crosson, Pierre (1987) Soil conservation and small watershed development. In T.J. Davis and I.A. Schirmer (eds) *Sustainability Issues in Agricultural Development: Proceedings of the Seventh Agricultural Sector Symposium*. Washington, DC: World Bank.

Davis, Ted J. and Schirmer, Isabel (1987) *Sustainability Issues in Agricultural Development: Proceedings of the Seventh Agricultural Sector Symposium*. Washington, DC: World Bank.

Dixon, John A., Talbot, Lee M. and LeMoigne, Guy J. (1989) *Dams and the Environment: Consideration in World Bank Projects*. Washington, DC: World Bank.

French, Hilary F. (1990) *Green Revolutions: Environmental Reconstruction in Eastern Europe and the Soviet Union*, Worldwatch Paper no. 99. Washington, DC: Worldwatch Institute.

Goldsmith, Edward and Hildyard, Nicholas (1984) *The Social and Environmental Effects of Large Dams*. San Francisco: Sierra Club Books.

Goodland, Robert, Asibey, E.O., Post, J. C. and Dyson, N.D. (1990) *Tropical Moist Forest Management: The Urgent Transition to Sustainability*. Washington, DC: World Bank.

Hertel, Skehuiu and Hertel, T.W. (1989) Deforestation and agricultural productivity in the Côte d'Ivoire. *American Journal of Agricultural Economics*, 71 (August), 703–11.

Krueger, Anne O., Michalopolous, Constantine and Ruttan, Vernon W. (1989) *Aid and Development*. Baltimore, MD: Johns Hopkins University Press.

Lele, Uma (1989) *Agricultural Growth, Domestic Policies, the External Environment Assistance to Africa: Lessons of a Quarter Century*, MADIA Discussion Paper no. 1. Washington, DC: World Bank.

Lele, Uma and Meyers, L. Richard (1989) *Growth and Structural Change in East Africa: Domestic Policies, Agricultural Performance, and World Bank Assistance, 1963–1986, Parts I and II*, MADIA Discussion Paper no. 3. Washington, DC: World Bank.

Lewis, Arthur W. (1954) Economic development with unlimited supplies of labor. *The Manchester School of Economic and Social Studies*, w/x(4), 1728–37.

Mikesell, Raymond F. and Williams, Lawrence F. (1992) *The International Banks and the Environment: From Growth to Sustainable Development – An Unfinished Agenda*. San Francisco: Sierra Club Books.

New York Times (1991) New effort would test possible coexistence of oil and rain forest. February 26.

Paglin, Morton (1965) Surplus agricultural labor and development: facts and figures. *American Economic Review*, 55 (September), 815–34.

Pingali, Prabhu, Bigot, Yves and Binswanger, Hans P. (1987) *Agricultural Mechanization and the Pollution of Farming Systems in Subsaharan Africa*. Baltimore, MD: Johns Hopkins University Press for the World Bank.

Repetto, Robert (1988) *Economic Policy Reform for Natural Resource Conservation*, Environmental Department Working Paper no. 4. Washington, DC: World Bank.

Repetto, Robert and Gillis, Malcolm (eds) (1988) *Public Policies and the Misuse of Forest Resources*. Cambridge: Cambridge University Press. (A World Resources Institute Book.)

Rich, Bruce M. (1990) Statement on behalf of the Environmental Defense Fund and National Wildlife Federation before the Subcommittee on Foreign Operations (mimeo). Washington, DC: Committee on Appropriations, US Senate, July 25.

Schultz, Theodore (1964) *Transforming Traditional Agriculture*. New Haven, CT: Yale University Press.

Solow, Robert M. (1957) Technical change and the aggregate production function. *Review of Economics and Statistics*, 39 (August), 312–20.

Svendsen, Mark and Meinzen-Dick, Ruth (eds) (1991) Sources of future growth in Indian irrigated agriculture. *Future Directions for Indian Agriculture: Research and Policy Issues*. Washington, DC: International Food Policy Research Institute.

World Bank (1989) *Sub-Saharan Africa from Crisis to Sustainable Growth: A Long-Term Perspective Study*. Washington, DC: World Bank.

World Bank (1990a). *Annual Report 1990*. Washington, DC: World Bank.

World Bank (1990b). *World Development Report*. New York: Oxford University Press.

4

Application of Sustainability to Development Policies

This chapter looks at several major policy categories found in textbooks or comprehensive treatises on development from the standpoint of how they might be altered to conform with the concept of sustainable development. The policies examined include those relating to economic growth, capital, economic liberalism versus government ownership and control, the use of common resources, development planning, and foreign trade and investment.

Little change is required in some conventional development policies to bring them into conformity with sustainable development, and in some cases sustainability provides an additional argument for the conventional position. For example, environmental economists usually favor the use of economic incentives over command and control for implementing social policies, and frown on trade and exchange controls and domestic price fixing that distorts the relationship between domestic and foreign prices and between domestic prices and costs. Such distortions often cause environmental damage by undervaluing natural resource products and discouraging investments that contribute to the sustainability of natural resources. Both sustainability and conventional development policy favor investment in human capital as contributing to productivity and social welfare. Both emphasize the promotion of research and the adoption of technology appropriate for dealing with specialized problems in agriculture, industry, and energy conservation. And both deplore fiscal deficits and excessive money expansion that lead to inflation, which inevitably distorts prices and misallocates resources.

Sustainable development differs from conventional development policy in several respects.¹ First, sustainable development tends to regard the natural resource base as the primary limiting factor of production, while conventional development emphasizes the availability of capital as the primary limiting factor. Moreover, there is only partial substitutability between natural resources and man-made capital, mainly because of our inability to substitute man-made capital for environmental assets, such as air and water. Second, sustainable development has adopted the ethical position that the natural resource base should be conserved to enable future generations to produce at least as much as the present generation. (Opinions on how much more it should be able to produce given technological progress differ among sustainable development economists.) Third, the value of all social benefits and all social costs, including natural resource depletion, must be included in the accounting system for measuring development performance. And fourth, waste absorption is a major function of the environment and an important limitation on economic growth.

In some areas the differences between sustainable development and conventional development are largely a matter of emphasis. Agriculture is given a special role in sustainable development (with less emphasis on industry), especially for promoting development in Third World countries. Capital is less important than natural resources, and sustainable development is not dependent on a high level of capital imports. The importance given to liberalizing foreign trade in modern conventional development economics is not shared by most environmentalists who see free trade areas and the General Agreement on Tariffs and Trade (GATT) as barriers to trade controls in the interest of environmental protection. Environmental planning is substituted for development planning and there is greater willingness to accept governmental controls over investment than is the case with conventional development economics. Finally, the advocacy of strong governmental controls on environmental protection and over the use of nearly all natural resources constitutes a countermovement against deregulation, which is currently favored by conventional development.

Policies for GDP Growth and for Sustainable Development

Despite the recognition in conventional development literature that the major goal of public policy should be development, the rate of growth in per capita gross domestic product (GDP) continues to be the standard by which policy success is measured and compared among countries. Sustainable development doctrine argues that GDP is not a proper measure of net economic progress because it includes natural resource depletion and degradation, and excludes many nonmarket social benefits and costs. Although there is a need for a comprehensive measure of market economic activity as provided by GDP, it does not serve well as a measure of development progress. Despite the difficulties in devising a measure that would command general agreement, such an index should be formulated and substituted for GDP in many applications.[2]

Sustainable development economists tend to be critical of conventional growth theories, but have not developed a quantitative theory of sustainable development, in part because of the absence of any single measure or combination of measures of the objective. It would also be exceedingly difficult to devise an objective function to explain such a heterogeneous or even nebulous outcome, especially since it might differ from country to country depending upon social preferences; for example, between marketable goods and services and nonmarketable amenities.

Conventional growth theory is usually limited to no more than three factor inputs with technological progress introduced as a homogeneous variable determining productivity or output per unit of inputs. None of the inputs in the equation is homogeneous and they need to be disaggregated before their respective contributions are measured. The natural resource factor is often omitted or simply treated as a constant. In the Cobb–Douglas production function, technology is a residual but often found to be responsible for half or more of the annual incease in output. Moreover, it is assumed that capital can be substituted for both resources and labor throughout the function. This is scarcely a useful theory of GDP growth. Human capital is usually neglected, as is the importance of interactions among the factor inputs. To formulate a theory of development we need to begin with a detailed analysis of all the elements contributing to performance, including not simply stocks of artificially defined factors, but also the policy framework in which the productive elements operate. This requires an intensive examination and statistical analysis of the experience of a large number of countries, from which might be distilled some useful theoretical insights.

In conventional development economics, macroeconomic policies are largely directed to maximizing GDP, and these policies in turn are heavily influenced by the prevailing theory of growth. Traditional development regarded the supply of capital as a major determinant of growth, since labor supply and natural resources were given in the intermediate run. Because the growth rate could be increased by capital imports or by increased domestic savings, policies were designed to promote these sources of investment capital. In recent years this approach has been modified and most development economists assign a more important role in accounting for growth to the quality and motivation of labor, the quality of entrepreneurship, the volume of R&D, and the political-economic framework within which all productive activity takes place. This approach is more difficult to model than one based largely on capital inputs, but provides the basis for a number of policies for promoting aggregate growth. It emphasizes expenditures for human capital and economic incentives for saving, investment, and R&D.

Since sustainable development lacks a single measurable economic objective and a theoretical model for achieving it, its policies are directed to a number of elements of social progress, of which per capita material betterment is only one. It places special emphasis on increasing human capital as both a means and an end of economic activity. Economic policies and programs that promote per capita GDP are not favored unless they promote social welfare and do not impair the natural resource base. For example, sustainable development economists judge the contribution of a billion-dollar multipurpose dam not simply in terms of the annual increase in agricultural and power output, but also in terms of its impact on the welfare of all individuals affected by the project, and insist on adherence to the principle of Pareto optimality. This doctrine, along with that of preserving natural resources for the use of future generations, is admittedly an ethical one. But they would argue that the goal of maximizing per capita GDP also reflects a social valuation, which they are not prepared to accept as the primary objective for economic policies.

The role of capital investment

In a recent article Lawrence Summers, Chief Economist of the World Bank, made the following statement regarding the allocation of capital in developing countries:

> Perhaps the most traditional role of government is investing in public goods – broadly defined – and getting as much return from those investments as possible. Helping governments make necessary infrastructure investment was, after all, an important rationale for the creation of the Bank. Economic logic suggests that the Bank's capital should be allocated to activities that produce the highest return. But that is not the way the Bank and other development institutions operate. Our portfolio is largely diversified, with investments in many sectors in most countries. Why? I fear that we practice a kind of diversification out of ignorance. Not knowing what types of projects have the highest returns, we invest in many different things as do our member governments.
>
> Yet, there is every reason to think there are large differences in the social rate of return to different types of project lending. The Bank's own operational evaluations suggest a large variation in the rate of return to projects in different sectors. . . . Of course, comparing bridges to power plants is like comparing apples and oranges. But seeking to compare their returns analytically must surely make more sense than investing in both to insure that the better one is included in the portfolio. (Summers, 1991, pp. 2–5)

Sustainable development economists fully agree with the above statement, but would add that it applies even more when the returns on projects take full account of environmental and resource costs. Many capital investments do not produce an addition to the net social product, or do not yield enough to cover the social opportunity cost of capital (i.e. net social returns from an alternative use of the capital). This is particularly true of projects that create environmental and natural resource damage, but it may also be true of subsidized housing projects for bureaucrats, or of flawed agricultural projects. A considerable portion of capital imports, whether in the form of low-interest loans by an external development assistance agency or of funds borrowed in the private international markets, makes little or no contribution to development. Capital inflow may simply increase consumption by particular groups or may be used for projects, such as military facilities, that do not enhance the social product. Therefore, sustainable development economists are not impressed by estimates of the flow of external assistance to developing countries, such as those compiled in the annual OECD *Development Cooperation Reports*. Capital inflows that fail to increase the net social product by an amount at least equal to the interest cost are a detriment to development. They increase the external debt without raising the net social product, after account is taken of the natural resource damage they generate.

Conventional development economics argues that capital is scarce in developing countries and, therefore, should earn a higher rate of return than it does in the industrial countries from which the capital is borrowed. It is also assumed that capital flows into the economic sectors and projects where it can produce the highest net economic returns. Capital supplied by MDBs is supposed to be directed into projects and sectors that will yield the maximum returns. To a very large degree, none of these assumptions is valid. In the private sectors of many developing countries capital is not scarce because there is little demand for it. Consequently, it is invested abroad. If there were significant opportunities for capital to earn higher returns in the country, it would not be exported; in many developing countries private capital exports run to many billions of dollars. Governments have an insatiable demand for capital for uneconomic uses generated by political motives. To a large degree, external development agencies respond to this demand, since it is the governments that do the borrowing and exercise considerable influence over the lending agencies.

Third World countries are currently burdened with massive external debt that most of them cannot service without drastic cuts in productive investment and social services. Many reasons are given for this condition, including declining raw material prices, world recessions, and oil shocks. But these events have characterized the world economy for many decades. The real reason for the debt problems is the failure to invest properly both imported capital and domestic saving. This failure has arisen in part from the way governments and external development agencies have allocated their capital and in part from price and other distortions created by inflation, the maze of government controls, and outright fraud. On the latter point, both conventional and sustainable development economists are now coming to an agreement.

Resource scarcity and growth

Traditional development economists have tended to minimize resource scarcity as a constraint on growth for two reasons. First, they point out that in a free market economy resources can never become scarce; they only become more expensive. Second, capital and technology can substitute for natural resources. There is considerable truth in both these statements. A high price for a particular natural resource, such as a mineral, stimulates exploration and development of technology for reducing extraction costs. Despite the enormous rise in output, the real price for nearly all minerals is lower today than 100 years ago. It is also possible to substitute capital investment in technology for natural resources: witness the substitution of optic fibers for copper and the nonmetallic compounds for a range of metals. The authors of *The Limits to Growth* (Meadows *et al.*, 1972), who forecast that growth would come to a halt because of natural resource scarcities by the year 2000, have been discredited. Even energy may one day become abundant when we learn to exploit solar energy more economically, or obtain energy from nuclear fusion.

There are, however, potential resource limitations on development that technology may not be able to overcome. There are natural resources for which we cannot substitute man-made capital embodying new technology. Such natural capital includes the atmosphere and the stratosphere, the oceans, wetlands, primary forests, watersheds, and fertile soil. Thus natural resources differ from variable inputs in the production function. They provide the environmental framework for all life. They are fixed in supply at least for several generations, and some are not renewable except over thousands of years once their functions are impaired. Their functions are impaired by waste flows in excess of their ability to absorb waste. This is true of the atmosphere, bodies of water, and the soil. Forests can be replanted, but replacing old-growth forests may require hundreds of years. However, by limiting waste flows and outright destruction of natural resources we can avoid the debasement of their functions so that they need not impair development. They are not exhausted in the same way that supplies of copper or iron ore are. In the case of forests or ocean fisheries, we must limit their use to the rate of replacement, but this would not impair general development. In the case of soil, it may be necessary to limit agricultural output in order to employ methods that will sustain fertility, but there are also ways to expand output by increasing productivity and restoring fertility to damaged soil.

Some natural resources provide direct utilities to humans as well as supporting life. There are really no man-made consumer goods that can substitute for these amenity services. Again, these natural resources do not wear out or exhaust their supplies in providing these amenities. However, their overuse by too many people wanting to enjoy them can reduce the value of their amenity services.

It is natural resources such as the atmosphere, the oceans, and primary forests that sustainable development economists are mainly concerned about, as contrasted with the natural resources for which man-made substitutes can be found through technological progress. Traditional development has paid little attention to this class of natural resources because it has not considered waste absorption to be an important element in the production process. Only recently have industrial firms been forced to develop procedures for disposing of, limiting, or recycling production waste, and for dealing with the problems of consumer waste generated by the users of their products. The production function has turned out to be circular, rather than linear with the consumer good as the end-product. Sustainable development theory corrects this oversight. The cycle must be completed by recycling or limiting the waste to the amount that the environmental resource can absorb.

Agricultural Policies

Agricultural sustainability is the most important message of sustainable development. Although there has been considerable loss of soil in the US farm belt as well as in other industrial countries, the loss of agricultural productivity of the land in the poor developing countries of Africa and Asia is becoming critical. Until the beginning of the present century, increases in agricultural output were primarily obtained by bringing new land into production, but nearly all the cultivatable land has now been occupied so that in the next century almost all increases in food production must come from higher yields per acre.

Before the Second World War, agriculture was largely ignored in development policy. The agricultural sector was relegated to supplying surplus labor, food for the urban sector, and foreign exchange from plantation exports – all devoted to industrial and urban development. A few development economists emphasized plantation exports as an engine of growth, but since plantations tended to be owned by foreign investors and were associated with colonialism, they were not a priority for development strategy by governments. Except for the construction of large irrigation dams, investment in agriculture did not loom large in national development plans or in the loan programs of the MDBs until the 1970s. Interest in agricultural development was initially influenced more by a desire to relieve poverty than for its contribution to growth. Agriculture did not rank with industry and infrastructure as harbingers of growth. During the 1980s and early 1990s the importance of agriculture in development policy increased rapidly in both the development literature and the loan programs of MDBs, but not in the politically influenced agenda of less developed country (LDC) governments.

There are several reasons for this new interest in agriculture. First is the emphasis on relieving world poverty expressed by humanitarian organizations and developed country governments. Closely associated has been dissatisfaction with the performance of the developing countries in improving the economic conditions of the rural sector. Development based on import-substituting industry, urban infrastructure, large government bureaucracies, state-owned industries, and wanton exploitation of natural resources has been a failure, with a legacy of large external debt, hyperinflation, capital flight, and little real growth. Another factor is the realization that in many developing countries not only was agricultural production inefficient, but the methods used contributed to a loss of natural resources.

Content of sustainable agriculture

Sustainable agriculture combines a positive role for agricultural production for growth with the objectives of poverty alleviation, natural resource conservation, and environmental protection. The strategic role of sustainable agriculture is revealed in the growing number of publications on the subject issued by MDBs, bilateral aid agencies, and academia. No other economic activity involves more people in the management of natural resources or generates a larger share of the physical product of low-income countries. Sustainable agriculture has two major objectives: (a) increasing the value of agricultural output, especially in poor countries; and (b) reducing adverse environmental impacts on the agricultural sector. The objective of raising world agricultural output in the context of an existing world surplus of agricultural products appears on the surface to be inconsistent. But this surplus is spurious in two senses. First, almost universal agricultural subsidies in developed countries have generated output in excess of full production costs, often at the expense of the natural resource base. Second, the world's poorest countries could readily consume the actual and potential surplus if they were able to produce and sell other goods and services in exchange for agricultural products. Hence, the problem of poor countries not being able to feed themselves adequately is basically a problem of poor productive capacity in both agricultural and nonagricultural sectors. Hong Kong and Singapore import large amounts of agricultural products, but they have a relatively high per capita foreign exchange income. In many developing countries, potential agricultural output is lost through government price controls and other policies that reduce production incentives and capital investment in agriculture. Thus, in some countries, agricultural output is low because of a variety of government activities. However, even in the absence of all harmful government intervention, many developing countries are faced with a rising demand exceeding the potential supply of agricultural products, and are unable to generate a surplus of nonagricultural goods with which to buy food and other essentials. Whether the solution for these countries lies in expanding agricultural output or in developing export industries depends upon the composition of their human and natural resources. In the short run, many poor countries must look to increasing their own food output, since building export capacity takes a long time.

Agricultural sustainability requires a technological approach

Scarcity of land and the need to intensify agricultural production to meet the growing demand for agricultural products require the rapid development and application of new technology for agriculture. The paradigm is found in the approach to industry, which emphasizes the application of technology appropriate to the labor, raw materials, and market opportunities in particular countries or regions. But intensive agriculture poses the additional problem of protecting the natural resource base, especially the soil and the quality and quantity of the water supply. Research and experimentation through pilot projects may be as important to agriculture as R&D is to industry. Moreover, much of the technology that works well in temperate zone industrial countries may not be appropriate for regions in the tropics. Certain types of programs favored by foreign assistance agencies, such as agricultural credits, should be abandoned or restructured in favor of research and technical training.

Research and technology orientation for agriculture is not the same as mechanization, which has sometimes proved costly and destructive of the soil. Nor does it necessarily require a large amount of imported inputs or expenditures of financial capital. Much of the capital for terracing, scientific application of irrigation water, and preparation of nonchemical fertilizers should represent the farmer's own labor. This saves financial capital and expands employment opportunities.

The introduction of agro-forestry may in some circumstances provide a solution to both the protection of the benefits of primary forests and the need for additional agricultural lands. It is clearly superior to slash and burn agriculture, and to large-scale conversion of primary forests for agricultural crops. A recent World Bank study (Nair, 1990, pp. 64–5) suggests that agro-forestry may be an answer to sustainability in land management in terms of the maintenance of soil productivity, watershed protection, and other benefits of forest ecosystems. Research and experimentation should play a role in determining the optimum combination of crops, trees, and planting arrangements for particular types of forest soils and climatic conditions.

There are a number of methodologies for increasing productivity in agriculture, including better tilling, various forms of irrigating, improving seeds, rotating crops, using fertilizers and pesticides, and crop and livestock systems (Reganold *et al.*, 1990). These and other methods have increased the productivity of Western agriculture enormously and have been responsible for the Green Revolution in parts of East Asia and other developing countries. The result has been an embarrassing surplus of agriculture production in the industrial countries and, with certain notable exceptions, a rapid rise in per capita food output and consumption in much of the Third World. But the outlook for sustainable agriculture in the next century is darkened by two factors. First, the productivity gains from the application of conventional technologies of the past century may not be sufficient to satisfy the increased demand in the next century for food, generated by a combination of population growth and increased per capita income in the developing countries. The rate of growth in demand in these countries ranges from 3 to 5 percent per year. The second factor is the environmental impact of agricultural intensification in the form of soil loss due to erosion, waterlogging and salinization, surface and groundwater pollution from fertilizers and pesticides, and the degradation of watersheds from rapid deforestation (Ruttan, 1991).

Agricultural optimists point to the decline in real prices for wheat since the middle of the nineteenth century and the decline in the real prices for rice and other foods since the middle of the twentieth century, despite rapid world population growth. They suggest that the ability of the world to feed itself after population has risen from five billion to perhaps ten or twelve billion (where, it is hoped, it will stabilize) may be extended by continued advances in molecular biology and genetic engineering applied to agricultural production. New technology may also be used to prevent the adverse environmental impacts on soil and water associated with intensive agricultural production. Technological optimists present doomsday forecasters with the fact that historical trends in productivity have overcome limited resources in the face of rising demand, and that technological advances are proceeding at an accelerated rate. Concern for sufficient food supplies, therefore, tends to be centered on the poorest of the developing countries, which also tend to have the highest population growth rates. Moreover, it is in these countries that soil erosion, deterioration of water quality and quantity and other environmental impacts have been greatest, and where there exist the greatest barriers to improving productivity or applying new technology. There may be a conflict between raising agricultural output to meet the demands of the present generation and the preservation of the agricultural resource base to meet the needs of future generations. It is conceivable that new technology can resolve this conflict by promoting both objectives. If so, the major barriers to sustainable development in Third World countries are social, institutional, and governmental.

State Control versus Free Enterprise

Conventional development economists favor free enterprise and private ownership, and are highly critical of the government domination of the economy that has characterized most developing countries since the Second World War. There are abundant examples of failures of state-dominated economies, and the bankruptcy of communism in Eastern Europe is viewed as a compelling argument for economic liberalism. The environmental movement is sometimes associated with a demand for increased government control, including over foreign trade and investment, and some environmentalists have contributed to this image by condemning large corporations and trade unions for destroying forests, creating shopping malls and suburban housing projects on wetlands and fragile coastal ecosystems, spoiling wildernesses with mining, and polluting the atmosphere with factories and vehicle traffic. The issue of government regulation presents a problem for sustainable development economists, many of whom also believe in the efficiency of economic competition, including free trade and incentives, and share the distrust of big government and state enterprise. Governments have also produced environmental and natural resource disasters. The dilemma arises in how to preserve a liberal economic order while at the same time preserving the natural resource base for future generations, and requiring private entities to take responsibility for the external diseconomies that they generate. As economies become more complex and interdependent, the impact of private activities on common environmental resources is more severe and threatening to the environmental foundation of the economic systems.

There is no way to reconcile private property and free enterprise with the requirements of sustainable development, except to treat the natural resources that are used by or affect the public as having the attributes of common goods. Private property owners must accept constraints on the use of environmentally sensitive assets, such as coastal lands, forests, wildlife habitat, and the shores of our lakes, rivers, and oceans. Limitations on private property rights are mandated by a number of federal and state laws concerning wetlands and endangered species, and there are a variety of local land-use planning regulations limiting construction to certain areas and felling trees. Most of these controls have been sanctioned by the courts, but their administration needs to be improved and standardized. Greater use needs to be made of positive and negative economic incentives, including fees, and, in some cases where special burdens are imposed, subsidies.

Property rights, externalities, and common resources

Technical external diseconomies, or the adverse effects of one economic agent's activities on other producers or consumers, have long been recognized in economic literature. It was the basis of the 'polluter pays' principle formulated by A. C. Pigou in his *Economics of Welfare* (1920). Conventional development has not fully embodied external diseconomies into social costs and the evaluation of development projects. Most external diseconomies arise because they affect the utilities provided by commonly used resources, such as the atmosphere, rivers, and lakes. However, there are some natural resources that are normally privately owned, but provide certain utilities to economic agents other than the owners. Good examples are forests and wetlands. Forests not only affect watersheds and even regional climates, but also have an influence on the global atmosphere and biodiversity, which provide global utilities. Wetlands help to purify water and provide a habitat for aquatic life and birds.

Conventional economics accepts the right of governments to control pollution and certain uses of lands having adverse effects on others, such as cutting trees in residential areas or failing to cut down unsightly weeds. In this way private property rights are limited. But there has been less acceptance of government control over the use of natural resources to protect utilities provided by private property that are commonly shared. To cite an example, a privately owned forest produces income to the owner from timber harvest, but the government may decide that the social benefits from leaving the forest in a natural state are greater than the private benefits from cutting the trees, and, therefore, prevents the owner from harvesting timber. In this case, the forest might be the habitat of an endangered species of bird, or mammal, or plant, survival of which is regarded as having a high social value. Since all natural resources provide some services that go beyond those to the individual owner, some would argue that all natural resources should be subject to strict governmental control, or even be government-owned and limited to uses imposed by the collective will. However, complete state control over uses of private property would be regarded as a serious limitation on private enterprise and freedom of the market, which many believe are necessary to maximize production of goods and services. Moreover, experience has shown that government ownership and control can be highly destructive of natural resources, and that the benefits from their use have often gone to state bureaucracies rather than to society as a whole. A serious problem for sustainable development is determining what uses of privately owned natural resources are important enough to be controlled by the state because of their contribution to the common good. Equally important is whether the state is exploiting natural resources in the public sector in a way that maximizes social benefits, as contrasted with using resources in a way that serves the interests of private industry (i.e. mining, timber, and cattle ranching).

The use of public lands

Many of the problems in preserving environmental assets concern the allocation and use of publicly owned property. Government land tends to be managed in the interest of particular industries and consumer groups, rather than in the public interest broadly conceived to include future generations. Some of the difficulty lies in the concept of what is in the public interest. Very often the public interest is identified with the economic welfare of certain communities, such as those depending heavily upon tourists who want to reside in hotels next to the beach, those whose economic livelihood depends upon building vacation homes in environmentally sensitive areas, or those whose workers are mainly employed in the lumber and forest products industries. Saving what little old-growth timber remains in the Pacific Northwest of the USA is opposed by legislators whose re-election depends on jobs generated by the lumber industry. Environmentally destructive dams are promoted by those who argue that the public interest requires the creation of jobs for the construction and associated industries. The amenity services of the environmental assets destroyed are enjoyed by a much larger public – hikers, birdwatchers, hunters, and fishermen. Speeches by Northwest legislators and bumper stickers proclaim that we should be saving jobs rather than spotted owls.

Most economists realize that what happens to jobs in particular industries does not determine the level of national employment. They also realize that work should be justified by producing things that people want, and that the purpose of economic activity is not job creation but consumer satisfaction. It would make more sense to pay workers to stay home rather than to pay them to destroy environmental resources. The overall level of employment in a country is determined by fiscal and monetary policies and by the cyclical behavior of the economy. Temporary unemployment is the price we pay for higher productivity in a free enterprise system, as contrasted with a socialist economy in which everyone is told where to work and what to produce.

Sustainable development economists believe that public lands should be allocated among alternative uses by determining the use that maximizes net social benefits in an intergenerational context. Since most land in public hands in the USA and Canada contains the last remaining primary forests, wetlands, and unspoiled scenic areas, preservation is greatly to be preferred to development. In the Pacific Northwest, environmentalists are divided between those who would stop all logging on publicly owned forest lands and those who would only terminate all logging on old growth forests. Thus far, no one has attempted a comprehensive social benefit–cost analysis of the two alternatives, but in any case environmental economists would not include the maintenance of employment as an objective in public land-use policy.

Allocation of public lands in developing countries, where substantial areas of publicly owned, uninhabited lands still exist, is somewhat different. Much of the land is in dense tropical forests, mountains, or deserts. Although preservation of all such land cannot be justified in terms of maximizing social welfare, great care needs to be exercised in its development if the long-run social costs are not to exceed the short-run economic benefits. This approach calls for planning, research, and experimentation rather than for opening the gates to massive migration.

Development Planning

During the 1950s and 1960s comprehensive development planning became very popular and the preparation of multi-year plans served to provide both a political document for Third World governments and an essential step in negotiating foreign aid. Plans were generally long on economic targets, such as the rate of growth of GDP and sectoral growth goals for industry, agriculture and infrastructure, but short on implementation. Except for projected expenditures of state enterprises and other government entities, the plans failed to show how the targets were to be achieved, and they were generally weak on policies to provide incentives to the private sector to realize investment and production objectives. Many of the targets, including GDP targets, were derived from capital-oriented growth models combined with macroeconomic analyses of saving, investment, and balance of payments deficits, to be covered by net capital inflow in the form of foreign aid and foreign private investment.

From the 1970s on, multi-year plans declined in popularity. While planning continued to be important in most developing countries, there was a greater emphasis on sectoral planning and the planning of large projects. One reason for the decline in comprehensive multi-year planning is that foreign aid agencies, such as USAID (which emphasized multi-year plans during the 1960s), were no longer impressed by the plans. Another reason was that successive failures of multi-year plans largely destroyed their political value for the government in power. Although the multilateral development banks continue to promote sectoral planning and detailed feasibility studies for projects they are asked to support, in recent years the major thrust of the external assistance agencies has been on reforming monetary, fiscal, trade, and foreign exchange policies. These agencies have also encouraged privatization of government enterprises and competitive markets as essential conditions for efficiency and growth.

Most advocates of sustainable development are generally in agreement with the trend away from comprehensive planning of economic activities and government ownership and control of agriculture and industry. The economic and environmental disasters in Eastern Europe have left few supporters of government-controlled agricultural communes and state industrial enterprises, or of state control of markets for commodities, services, and credit. Experience with socialist economies has shown that governments cannot be trusted to control pollution created by the economic activities they own and direct. Governments can do a better job of requiring private firms to internalize their environmental impacts. Governments can also provide economic incentives for pollution abatement in the form of taxes and marketable permits where private firms are operating in competitive markets. Governments of developed and developing countries continue to own and control a large proportion of the natural resources – forests, rivers, lakes, wetlands, minerals in the subsoil, and coastal areas. They control the 'commons' – the atmosphere, waterways, and groundwater. Moreover, even where some of these resources are privately owned, governments traditionally have taken responsibility for their use and exploitation because of the impacts of natural resources on social welfare and national security. For these reasons sustainability economists who favor comprehensive natural resource planning as a legitimate and necessary governmental activity are not outside the mainstream of planning. But their agenda is oriented to resource conservation and environmental protection rather than to the maximization of economic growth. Given the objectives of sustainable development, natural resource accounting and planning are important for shaping governmental policies for achieving the objectives. The most common objectives for natural resource management are to keep the flow of waste well within the limits of the absorptive capacity of the environment, to prevent continuous net depletion of renewable resources, and to limit the depletion of exhaustible resources to amounts that can be offset by substitution and increased efficiency of resource use. These objectives are designed to enable future generations to maintain or expand output without meeting a waste absorption or natural resource constraint.

Shaping governmental policies to achieve these objectives requires natural resource accounting and resource planning. Any economic activity gives rise to natural resource depletion and waste flows into the environment. Certain types of economic activity, such as reforestation and crop rotation, restore renewable resources, while new technology and changes in existing technology can reduce waste flows into the air, water, and soil, or conserve natural resource inputs by increasing the efficiency of their production or use. Environmental and resource planning must be based on a system of accounts that will enable government officials to determine the environmental and resource impacts of past economic activities, such as the consumption of energy and nonfuel resources, soil depletion, and the lowering of groundwater levels. Baseline projections can then be made on the effects of projected economic activities, assuming no change in governmental policy or in technology. Examples might be the accumulation of greenhouse gases for the projected level of manufacturing activity, the loss of topsoil on farmland, or the amount of deforestation. A system of natural resource accounts has been formulated by environmental economists and accounts have been constructed in a few countries.[3] National resource plans can then be formulated for altering the environmental and natural resource impacts of projected economic activity. The plans can be designed to meet feasible environmental targets, say by 2000, 2010, or later. The setting of targets requires tradeoffs between production and environmental and resource objectives. The plans would consist of pollution abatement programs, government-sponsored R&D, technical assistance to farmers, and management programs for government-owned resources. Plans can be national, or global for dealing with the world environment.

The advantages of national or global natural resource planning over project or sector resource planning are that the former take account of the multiple impacts of particular economic activities on environmental resources and the interactions among environmental assets. Thus, the exhaustion of petroleum reserves may mean a greater use of coal, which creates greater adverse environmental impacts. This in turn increases the social benefits of developing renewable sources of energy. Models of global warming enable countries to estimate the costs of adapting to higher temperatures as against the costs of slowing down the accumulation of greenhouse gases. Decisions on pollution abatement ought to be made in the light of projections of pollution impacts several decades in the future.

Despite the advantages of comprehensive natural resource accounting and planning, national and global planning on a broad scale is not likely to occur for many decades. However, regional resource planning oriented to specific projects or programs is becoming increasingly important in developing countries. One reason is that in order to obtain external assistance for large projects, governments are required to prepare comprehensive EIAs that cover all the direct and indirect impacts of the projects, together with plans for mitigating these impacts. An EIA for a large multipurpose dam involves dozens of categories of impacts that may affect the economic activities and social welfare of millions of people in regions covering thousands of square miles. This type of project and program planning goes well beyond conventional economic feasibility studies required by MDBs.

Environmental action plans

Beginning in 1990, the World Bank requested that its low-income members (who are eligible for IDA loans) prepare environmental action plans (EAPs) in cooperation with Bank staff members. EAPs that have been completed have not been made public, but I have reviewed a number of them under contract with the Bank. The general guidelines for the EAPs provide for an analysis of the country's overall economic situation and development strategy, and an identification and description of the major environmental and natural resource problems in the country. On the basis of this analysis, EAPs make specific recommendations for policy change, investment, research, and the institutional strengthening required for dealing with environmental issues.

The best of the EAPs reviewed are excellent examples of how plans for the solution of environmental and resource management problems can be integrated with economic development strategies at the sectoral and project-specific level. For example, countries faced with soil degradation need to adjust their agricultural programs and projects to deal specifically with the causes of degradation, while urban development programs need to address urban pollution in all its forms as an integral part of the programs.

The EAPs are also supposed to formulate projects and programs suitable for World Bank Group financing and to establish priorities for these projects, again combining the objectives of economic growth with environmental improvement and sustainable resource management. In some cases, the EAPs cover a large number of measures in a variety of economic sectors that do not constitute specific projects of the type normally financed by the Bank. Nevertheless, they involve substantial government expenditures for which government revenues are not available. Hence, in some instances the government has been encouraged to prepare a comprehensive plan and to request an environmental adjustment loan which would cover fiscal requirements for a large number of actions. It would seem desirable for the Bank to consider making such loans as a part of its structural adjustment loan program.

Foreign Trade and Investment

Most conventional economists regard free trade as a positive influence on economic growth. Not only should developing countries avoid trade restrictions on their residents, but free world trade is essential for providing markets for Third World exports and maximizing their long-run terms of trade. The argument that free trade is good for development has in the past been generally rejected by governments of developing countries and by many development economists. Recently, some Third World governments have become convinced of the desirability of abandoning controls on foreign trade and have been taking an interest in the GATT, which they had previously ignored. One reason is that they have come to see the GATT as an instrument for opening markets in the industrial countries for their products.

Developing countries have used discriminatory controls on foreign direct investments during much of the post-Second World War period. Multinational mineral firms have been accused of exploiting their natural resources, while multinational industrial firms have allegedly driven domestic firms out of business and overcharged for imports. A few developing countries are beginning to liberalize their regulations on foreign investment as well as relaxing import and export controls. In doing so they have been responding to advice from the World Bank, the IMF, USAID, and other external assistance agencies. The United Nations agencies, which previously favored trade and foreign investment controls by developing countries, have changed their counsel in favor of liberalized trade and investment policies.

Some environmentalists have a different message on the desirability of free trade and investment, a message that has been directed to the governments of both developing and industrial countries. Basically it is that liberalized foreign trade and investment interferes with national measures to protect the environment and to conserve natural resources. It is argued that pollution controls on domestic production may be undermined by imports from countries where no controls exist, and multinational firms may escape domestic controls by moving into 'pollution havens,' thereby creating a demand to relax domestic controls. Conservation groups throughout the world have blamed much of the destruction of tropical forests, birds, animals, and indigenous peoples on the production of petroleum, minerals, and timber by multinational firms. Investments by US firms on the Mexican side of the border have been blamed for the deplorable environmental conditions created by the *maquilladora* plants. Some of the pollution has spilled over into the USA. Consequently, US conservation groups have either opposed the negotiation of the North American Free Trade Area (NAFTA), or demanded that the NAFTA treaty be accompanied by an agreement requiring participating countries to adopt environmental standards equal to or stricter than US standards. They have also been very critical of the GATT because it lacks certain exceptions to free trade rules regarded as essential for protecting the environment and natural resources. In August 1991 the Sierra Club, in association with two other NGOs, brought suit against the US Trade Representative (USTR) on grounds that the USTR had undertaken negotiations for the NAFTA and under the Uruguay Round of the GATT without filing an environmental impact statement (EIS), which they allege is required by the National Environmental Policy Act (Sierra Club, 1991).

Environmentalists have also demanded import restrictions on commodities produced under conditions that damage the global environment, including threatened or endangered species. Thus, environmental groups have demanded restrictions on imports of tropical woods and the furs and skins of certain animals. These and other environmentally related trade restrictions are alleged to conflict with GATT 'fair trade' rules. For example, in August 1991 a GATT panel decided against a US action restricting imports of tuna from countries whose fishermen violate US standards for netting tuna in a manner that protects dolphins from being trapped (GATT, 1991, p. 2). Environmentalists also demand that capital exporting countries establish controls over their foreign investments to prevent investors from degrading natural resources in the host countries.

Most environmental economists are in accord with modern conventional development thought in favoring free markets for commodities, foreign exchange, and foreign trade. However, they do advocate government intervention for environmental pollution abatement and natural resource conservation. In doing so, they prefer economic incentives in the form of fees and subsidies over command and control methods, or price controls. For example, where possible they advocate penalty fees or marketable permits for inducing compliance with pollution standards, or subsidies based on performance to induce conservation. Although they generally favor free foreign trade, including the negotiation of free trade areas (FTAs), as means of promoting Third World development, they have insisted on trade controls for preventing imports from undermining national environmental and resource conservation measures.

The apparent conflict between environmentalism and the liberalization of world trade and investment presents a challenge to environmental economists who must show how these two objectives can be made compatible. Now that most development economists have come to believe that free trade and investment are compatible with, and perhaps essential to, economic growth, it would be unfortunate if free trade and capital movements were now rejected on environmental grounds. Some changes do need to be made in the GATT trade rules to recognize environmental safeguards. Few people were conscious of such problems when the GATT was first negotiated in 1947 (US Department of State, 1950). The GATT should make clear that every member has a right to protect its consumers by restricting imports that conflict with regulations on domestic products, as long as the regulations do not discriminate between imports and domestic goods. Harmonization of standards among imports for GATT members may be feasible in some cases, but not in others. During the Uruguay Round, the USTR made an effort to amend the GATT to require members to apply uniform sanitation standards for imported foods and drugs, with the standards to be determined by an international agency, such as the CODEX Alimentarius Commission. Quantitative import restrictions that are not in conformity with the 'scientific evidence' established by recognized international research agencies would be regarded as being in violation of the GATT. However, this was strongly opposed by environmental organizations on the grounds that federal and state sanitation regulations on domestic products might be more strict and, therefore, imports under an international agency standard might undermine the government's statutory powers.

It would be difficult and perhaps impossible to obtain unanimous acceptance of any uniform standard. Even within the European Community (EC), where an effort has been made to achieve harmonization of both consumption and production standards on a large number of commodities entering into EC trade, there have been substantial difficulties in achieving harmonization. The best approach may be to allow each member of the GATT to enforce its own standards on imported products and to provide for dispute settlement solely on questions of whether the standards applied to imported products are more strict than those applied to domestic products.

The issue of whether GATT members should be able to impose restrictions on imports whose production is regarded as having an adverse impact on the global environment or on environmental conditions in the producing country is much more controversial. This issue not only involves damage to endangered species and destruction of tropical rainforests, but may eventually involve the emission of greenhouse gases should an international agreement on such emissions be achieved. It might arise if the US government or the state of New York were to restrict imports of electric power produced in Quebec by the environmentally flawed James Bay Project. To allow each importing country to impose its own production standards on all imports could endanger the viability of the GATT and pose a serious obstacle to the negotiation of FTAs. It is suggested that restrictions on production in the interest of the environment be limited to those cases where there is an international convention on environmental conditions of production, and that the sanctions imposed be established by an international convention. The GATT rules should permit such internationally imposed sanctions, but the GATT itself is scarcely the instrument for determining environmental standards.

FTAs involving both developed and developing countries can provide an important stimulus to foreign investment and to the export earnings of the developing country members. Despite the interest of environmentalists in promoting Third World development, most US environmental groups have opposed the NAFTA, largely on the grounds that it would increase pollution-creating activities in the US–Mexico border area and would undermine US environmental regulations by inducing US firms to move south of the border. Some US environmental groups would not be willing to approve the NAFTA unless it required environmental standards in Mexico to be as strict as those in the USA. However, other members of the NAFTA, including Canada, are unlikely to accept all US environmental standards. To allow individual members unilaterally to establish production standards for imports from other members is likely to generate trade disputes that would endanger the existence of the Agreement.

Most environmental economists are convinced that the NAFTA would improve Mexico's economy and eventually promote environmental improvement in that country. However, they are faced with the problem of how trade and investment can be liberalized without increasing environmental damage in the USA from US–Mexico border activities. The solution to the problem may be the establishment of a joint commission (appointed by all three NAFTA members) to formulate and enforce environmental standards for the border area.

Complete freedom to restrict imports on environmental grounds would probably make the GATT or any FTA unworkable. On the other hand, both the GATT and the NAFTA should recognize the right of countries to require imported products to meet their domestic product standards and to take measures to conserve their natural resources, even though such actions are an obstacle to international trade.

Population and Development

Twentieth-century development economists reject the Malthusian view of population growth as a barrier to increasing per capita income, and some have viewed population growth as a stimulant to economic growth. Most either deny that a high rate of population growth retards per capita income growth, or maintain that neither economic logic nor statistical analysis supports a negative relationship.[4] A major canon of the sustainable development doctrine is that population growth is the greatest threat to sustainable development, and perhaps to the survival of the human species. One of the consequences of population growth is crowding, which reduces the quality of life; the quality of life is not reflected in per capita GDP.

This view is not necessarily based on the inability of society to increase output with continued population growth, but on the inability of the environment to absorb the wastes associated with an indefinitely expanding population. This position shifts the argument from the possibility of increasing or maintaining gross per capita output to that of maintaining net per capita output after environmental resource depletion and degradation. Sustainable development economists argue that although technological advances may overcome natural resource scarcities for expanding the output of goods and services, they will not save the world from drowning in its wastes. Unless population levels off fairly soon, the excess of waste generated over waste absorbed will reach a threshold beyond which equilibrium can never be restored. This view is, of course, highly controversial since capital and technology can be shifted to reducing waste and promoting waste absorption at the cost of output growth. The real problem may be the political will and the governmental wisdom to take action in time. On the other hand, technology cannot overcome a reduction in the quality of life that would accompany a doubling in the size of our cities, perpetual traffic jams on the highways, and overcrowding of our beaches and natural recreation areas.

Most development economists agree on the necessity of stemming population growth in poor developing countries with very limited land and other resources. For the sub-Saharan countries, technology and foreign capital cannot offset the rapid decline in soil productivity and the spread of desertification unless population is brought under control. In these countries, per capita agricultural output has been declining for the past two decades, while population has been growing at 2–3 percent per annum. Despite the recent improvement in agricultural production, the Indian subcontinent could be headed for economic disaster before population levels off in accordance with current demographic predictions. Hence, birth control programs may be the most urgent form of foreign aid. Unfortunately, even if the international economic assistance agencies and the governments of developing countries are willing to give family planning the highest priority, the sociological barriers to reducing birth rates radically may be too great for any amount of external assistance to have a significant impact. Higher per capita incomes and the liberation of women are the answers, but in many societies these may require several generations.

Education and Human Resources

Traditional development has emphasized investment in economic activities, such as agriculture, industry, and infrastructure, as the primary contributors to growth and development. Such investments, together with technological advances, are the prime movers in the growth models that explain real per capita GDP. Investments in education and human capital were not included, and the goods and services required to carry out these activities were regarded as consumption. In recent decades, conventional economists have recognized these expenditures as investments in human capital.

Environmental economists regard expenditure for human resources as a greater contribution to social output than investment in man-made capital. The products of such investments are the content of development as contrasted with economic growth. Education, health, sanitation, and personal safety not only make a contribution to the social product, but also produce social benefits that are just as important to living as bread, wine, and cars.

Most conventional development economists do not deny that non-marketed social benefits are a part of development. However, they would argue that to have development there must be growth in the measurable output of goods and services, since without growth consumption in the form of public expenditures on education and human resources cannot increase. Since sustainable development economists do not deny the need to increase output and productivity, the differences in policies between the two groups are mainly a matter of emphasis and the priorities given to various social benefits.

Summary

While conventional and environmental economists are broadly in agreement on market incentives as contrasted with direct controls and price fixing for achieving social objectives, they differ either in emphasis or fundamentally on a number of development policies. Environmental economists are critical of many conventional policies for promoting GDP growth because they reject the traditional concept of growth as a basic social goal. Sustainable development encompasses a combination of social values usually included in social and economic progress plus elements of sustainability, which environmental economists themselves differ over. Since they regard the natural resource base as the limiting factor in expanding the net domestic product, they tend to reject capital-based growth models. Therefore, they regard allocation of capital among alternative uses, including social programs and environmental and resource conservation, to be much more important than the total volume of capital available for development. The absence of a macroeconomic theory or quantitative objective function makes for a conglomeration of policies directed toward a multiplicity of loosely related social objectives. Although conventional economic development has accommodated a number of social objectives, such as the elimination of poverty, universal education and health services, and environmental protection, the realization of these goals is dependent upon economic growth. Sustainable development, on the other hand, has no primary quantitative goal, but rather advocates a number of specific social objectives, many of which are nonquantitative.

These differences in goals and policy orientation are revealed in the differences with respect to the issues discussed in this chapter. Capital and technology are not allocated to agriculture to enhance the contribution of agriculture to overall economic growth, but rather for poverty alleviation, social equity for the rural sector, and conservation of resources. Likewise, the uses of public land should not be determined by the contribution of lumber and minerals to GDP, but by the maximization of net social benefits, which include many values not found in conventional national product accounts.

In the next chapter I review the extent to which external assistance agencies have implemented the elements of sustainable development and the impact of their acceptance of environmental values on lending operations.

NOTES

1 For a review of the content of sustainable agricultural development, see Davis and Schirmer (1987) and Faeth *et al.* (1991).
2 The Human Development Index (HDI) formulated by the UNDP combines

real national income with social indicators, such as adult literacy and life expectancy. It is not an absolute measure, but simply an indicator of HDI rank from Japan, which had the highest value in 1990, to Sierra Leone, with the lowest ranking (UNDP, 1991, pp. 15–20). The high weight given to GDP per capita income makes the index inappropriate from the standpoint of sustainable development economics. Also, GDP rankings are quite different when currency values reflect relative purchasing power rather than exchange market prices. For example, real per capita GDP comparisons based on purchasing power parities show that in 1988 the USA had the highest in the world, followed by Switzerland, Japan, and France (Summers and Heston, 1988, 1991).

3 For a description of natural resource accounting systems in France and Norway, see Pearce *et al.* (1989, Chapter 4).

4 In early additions to his text, the *Economics of Development*, Everett Hagen strongly denied that high population growth retarded development, but in a more recent edition he regards the argument on either side of the issue to be inconclusive (Hagen, 1986, pp. 350–2).

REFERENCES

Davis, Ted J. and Schirmer, Isabel A. (eds) (1987) *Sustainable Issues in Agricultural Development: Proceedings of the Seventh Agricultural Sector Symposium.* Washington, DC: World Bank.

Faeth, Paul, Repetto, Robert, Croll, Kim, Qi Dai and Helmers, Glenn (1991) *Paying the Farm Bill: US Agricultural Policy and the Transition to Sustainable Agriculture.* Washington, DC: World Resource Institute.

GATT (1991) *Focus* (GATT Newsletter), no. 78, January/February.

Hagen, Everett E. (1986) *The Economics of Development*, 4th edn. Homewood, IL: Irwin.

Meadows, Donella, Meadows, Dennis, Randers, Jorgen and Behrens, William, III (1972) *The Limits to Growth.* New York: Universe Books.

Nair, E.K.R. (1990) *Prospects of Agroforestry in the Tropics*, Technical Paper no. 131. Washington, DC: World Bank.

Pearce, David, Markandya, Anil and Barbier, Edward B. (1989) *Blueprint for a Green Economy.* London: Earthscan Publications.

Pigou, A.C. (1920) *Economics of Welfare.* London: Macmillan.

Reganold, J.P., Papandick, R.I. and Parr, J.R. (1990) Sustainable agriculture. *Scientific American*, June.

Ruttan, Vernon W. (1991) Sustainable growth in agricultural production: poverty, policy and science (unpublished paper prepared for International Food Policy Research Institute Seminar on 'Agricultural Sustainability, Growth and Poverty Alleviation'). Feldafing, Germany, September 23–27.

Sierra Club (1991) Sierra Club files lawsuit against US Trade Representative over compliance with National Environmental Policy Act. Press release, Sierra Club, Washington, DC, August 1.

Summers, Lawrence (1991) Research challenges for development economists. *Finance and Development*, September, 2–5.

Summers, Robert and Heston, Alan (1988) A new set of international comparisons of real product and price levels: estimates for 130 countries, 1950–1985. *Review of Income and Wealth*, **34**(1) (March), 1–26.

Summers, Robert and Heston, Alan (1991) The pan-world table (Mark V): an expanded set of international comparisons, 1950–1988. *Quarterly Journal of Economics*, **106**. 2.

UNDP (1991) *Human Development Report*. New York: Oxford University Press.

US Department of State (1950) *The General Agreement on Tariffs and Trade (Amended Text)*. Washington, DC: US Government, February.

5

Sustainable Development and the Foreign Assistance Agencies

Background

The policies of external assistance agencies have been strongly influenced by traditional development theory. However, foreign aid strategies and development policies have in considerable measure been shaped by the external agencies themselves. In the period just after the Second World War, per capita growth was virtually the only recognized measure of progress, and the dominant explanation for growth was capital investment. During the 1950s and early 1960s, bilateral development assistance was several times larger than multilateral development assistance, with USAID by far the leading source. In the first half of the 1960s, US foreign aid policy was heavily influenced by capital-oriented growth models based on the so-called Harrod–Domar model.[1] According to this model, the rate of growth in output is a function of the ratio of investment to output and the incremental capital–output ratio (ICOR). Investment is equal to domestic savings plus net capital imports. If a country is investing (and saving) 9 percent of its GDP and ICOR is 3, its rate of growth will be 3 percent per annum. If the country receives a flow of external aid equal to 3 percent of GDP, it can grow at a rate of 4 percent. Therefore, with the help of external assistance, an economy can grow at a faster rate than that permitted by its domestic savings alone. Moreover, if the marginal propensity to save is greater than the average propensity, the savings ratio will rise as income rises, so that increased domestic saving can substitute for the external capital supplement to investment. Thus, given the critical flow of external capital, aid can be tapered off and a higher rate of growth can be sustained by internal savings alone.

The leading growth theories of the 1950s and 1960s supported the position that to achieve a certain rate of increase in per capita output there must be a specific annual inflow of foreign aid. Those theories were quite popular with developing country representatives in the UN, who lobbied for a large flow of development aid. A report by a group of experts appointed by the UN Secretary General (United Nations, 1951, pp. 75–9) estimated that an annual flow of $14 billion ($61 billion in 1990 prices) in external capital to the developing countries would be required to support an average 2 percent rate of growth in their per capita national income over the 1950–60 period. Such estimates became the basis for an effort in the UN to establish a large trust fund to be contributed by the developed countries for making grants to developing countries. The idea that transferring large amounts of capital to poor countries will somehow promote their development on a sustainable basis remains popular in many developing countries to this day. Most developing countries would like to have access to large amounts of capital without conditions on its use. This approach is contrasted with project loans made by the MDBs and with structural adjustment loans (SALs) to which conditions regarding government policies are attached.

The World Bank, which became the world's largest development lender in the 1970s, initially made loans to developing countries only for specific projects, mainly for infrastructure. Owing to the conservative orientation of its early presidents and to a limited interpretation of the Bank's Articles of Agreement (which later came to be interpreted more liberally), the Bank did not regard itself as a development institution. Rather, it viewed itself as a supplier of 'bankable' credits for specific projects on application from potential borrowers, similar to a private investment bank, which has no special responsibility for the overall welfare of its borrowers. The Bank eschewed any formal growth model as a guide to its loan operations in a country, but emphasized financial stability and 'capital absorptive capacity' (or the ability to make efficient use of capital) as primary conditions for creditworthiness. During the presidency of Robert McNamara (1968–80) the Bank greatly expanded the volume of its loans and the variety of activities that it supported. In financial year (FY) 1964 transportation and power accounted for 85 percent of the Bank's loans, while only 3 percent supported agriculture, with almost no loans going for social programs such as education, sanitation, and health. In 1961 the International Development Association (IDA) was established as an affiliate of the Bank to make loans on generous or nonconventional terms (no interest and 40-year repayment) to poor countries with limited ability to repay foreign debt.[2] In FY 1972, loans to agriculture by the World Bank and IDA were about 15 percent of total loans, and loans for social projects, such as education and population planning, amounted to over 9 percent.

As the World Bank Group (which includes the Bank, the IDA and the

International Finance Corporation (IFC)[3]) increased its concern for the development progress of its members, it became interested in the environmental impacts associated with its loans. This was a natural evolution since the environmental impacts of development activities give rise to social costs and benefits, which are included in development but not necessarily a part of growth. The Bank's interest in the environment was reflected in statements by President McNamara, who appointed the Bank's first environmental advisors in 1970 and established an Office of Environmental Affairs in 1973. But there was little effort to formulate environmental standards or tie them to the Bank's lending operations until the latter part of the 1980s.

Following a suit by conservation organizations in which it was alleged that USAID had failed to comply with the National Environmental Policy Act (NEPA), which requires preparation of an EIS for all US government-financed projects, USAID began requiring the preparation of an EIS for each of its foreign aid projects. In 1978 the US Foreign Assistance Act was amended specifically to require USAID to prepare an EIS for its projects, together with evaluations of developing countries' environmental and resource problems.

Currently all multilateral development banks to which the US government makes a financial contribution require that an environmental impact assessment (EIA) be prepared for projects they finance, unless a preliminary investigation shows that there are no environmental impacts associated with the project.[4] This applies to the World Bank Group, the Inter-American Development Bank (IADB), the Asian Development Bank (ADB), and the African Development Bank (AfDB). The almost universal adoption of the EIA and the application of environmental standards to all externally assisted development projects and programs was in large measure the result of actions by the US Congress promoted by US conservation organizations. Although US government representatives on the boards of directors of MDBs do not have a veto over the loans of these banks, by law they are required to vote against loans for projects if specific environmental procedures are not followed.[5] Since the MDBs are heavily dependent on the US government for increases in their capital, they have a special incentive to comply with these procedures.

MDB Environmental Impact Assessment Procedures

The EIAs and other procedures that MDBs are expected to follow to ensure that projects financed by their loans do not impair the environment constitute a major intrusion into the economic activities of their client countries. The traditional project loan appraisal is concerned with (a) engineering feasibility, including reliability and productive life of the project, and (b) financial feasibility. Financial feasibility is determined by an estimate of the probability adjusted annual rate of return on capital investment in the project. The EIA adds a third category of feasibility: it identifies the direct and indirect environmental or natural resource impacts of the project, investigates how these impacts could be avoided or mitigated, and makes recommendations for improving the environmental feasibility or terminating the project. There are no generally accepted quantitative standards for environmental feasibility as there are for engineering and financial feasibility. Final decisions are made on the basis of broad judgements balancing nonquantitative social benefits against social costs. However, the investigation and analysis required for EIAs can be quite sophisticated and involve scientific methodology. EIAs for large and complex projects require engineering, biological, ecological, and economic studies that may cost several million dollars and require the services of specialists in several fields.

Ideally, the EIA process should take place in parallel with engineering and financial feasibility studies and have a substantial impact on the final project design. Frequently, however, the EIA is conducted after the project design is completed, and the environmental team is under pressure to avoid recommending major changes in the basic plan. In this case, the EIA may become little more than a basis for an EIS that throws a favorable light on the environmental consequences of the project. Where the EIA is an integral part of the planning process and has an influence on each stage of the project design, adjustments can be made to minimize or avoid adverse environmental impacts. At each stage the environmental impacts need to be identified and measured and alternative modifications considered. EIAs should also estimate environmental costs associated with the project that are not included in the actual monetary outlays. Such information provides a basis for a full social benefit–cost accounting, on which final approval should be made.

A number of guidelines for the preparation of EIAs have been published by international organizations (see, for example, UNESCAP, 1985). The following outline summarizes the basic elements included in most of them:

1   Environmental impacts should be identified before the completion of the preliminary design of the project. This process identifies problems likely to be significant and to require special study. If no significant impacts are found, a decision may be made that no EIA is necessary, or that a full EIA need not be performed.
2   A baseline study should be prepared, projecting environmental changes likely to occur in the absence of the project and those likely to occur with the project.
3   An evaluation of the environmental impacts on humans, natural resources, production, ecology, social organizations, and cultures should be prepared and to the maximum extent possible converted into monetary costs.
4   Mitigation measures should be determined for the environmental impacts indicated in (3), together with cost estimates of mitigation measures.
5   Comparison of the costs of alternative measures for mitigating environmental

impacts with the benefits of those measures should be made, using benefit–cost analysis, in preparation of the final project design. The alternatives should include entirely different projects with less harmful environmental impacts or no project.

6 An EIA should be made available to officials responsible for the final approval of the project or for a loan for the project. A detailed summary (if not the entire EIA) should be made available to the public well before approval of the project or loan.

7 Environmental impacts should be monitored throughout the project construction period. If necessary, changes should be recommended to conform with the expectations of the EIA.

8 There should be post-construction monitoring of the project with periodic reports.

Environmentalists have welcomed the adoption of EIAs by the MDBs, but the above guidelines leave many of their questions unanswered. One question is how the investigation of the environmental impacts, the social costs of the impacts, and the costs of mitigation influence the decisions on the final project design and its approval for construction or financing by a lending institution. No matter how carefully and objectively an EIA is performed, it does not provide a formula for dealing with the problems that are discovered during the investigation. Statements such as 'we take adequate account of environmental impacts' do not provide a basis for objective judgement on the environmental feasibility of a project. Only by rigorous analysis of the social benefits and costs is it possible to reach scientifically objective conclusions. It is important to know whether the final decision on the project is made on the basis of a full social benefit–cost analysis in which environmental costs that are not a part of the monetary expenditures on the project are included. Currently MDBs do not include all environmental costs in EIAs, or require them to be included by the government of the borrowing country, which normally prepares an EIA.

A second question is whether sustainability criteria are included in the EIA. This would require that any resource depletion caused by construction and operation of a project be treated as a social cost. Currently, this is not done in EIAs prepared for projects financed by MDBs.

A third question is whether adequate account is taken of risk in estimating social benefits and costs. Resource projects, such as multiple purpose dams and mines, are especially vulnerable to environmental disasters, so that social costs should include an allowance for such possibilities. These include not only collapse of a dam, but also unforeseen environmental impacts of a dam, such as downstream pollution.

A fourth question concerns whether the project will be completed, operated, and maintained in accordance with the project design that is supposed to take full account of the environmental impacts identified by the EIA. This question is exceedingly important since many of the projects financed by MDBs that have proved to be environmentally flawed became so because of the government's failure to fulfill the loan conditions. Alternatively, the EIA may not have foreseen some of the environmental problems associated with the project.

EIAs and sustainability

An EIA may identify all the environmental impacts of a project, provide reliable estimates of their full social costs, and yet not embody the principle of sustainability. Conventional project evaluation is concerned with the *net* social benefits to the present generation. This is a consequence of the practice of discounting future costs and benefits at the social rate of discount, which is essential for analyzing benefits and costs that are realized in different time frames – they must all be adjusted to present values. As is noted in earlier chapters, discounting discriminates against future generations in the sense that the costs a project might impose on people living 50 years from now are assigned a very low value. An example might be the cost of cleaning up a nuclear plant site at the time of dismantling, say 30 years from now. If this cost is estimated at $10 million, the present value is only $570,000, assuming a 10 percent discount rate. Yet the $10 million must be paid by a future generation, which may get little benefit from the plant. There could be a similar cost at the end of the useful life of a multipurpose dam that is expected to silt up at the end of 50 years, after which the dam must be torn down and the river restored to its previous course. If these termination costs were internalized year after year and deducted from the benefits when calculating the present value of the project, the project might not have been built, or if it were, the annual benefits would have been reduced each year by an amount which, when saved and compounded at the discount rate, would provide a fund sufficient to pay the termination costs. The same procedure was suggested in Chapter 2 for applying the principle of sustainability to projects that deplete natural resources or deteriorate their quality so that their productivity is reduced. Thus, in order to apply sustainability to the EIA process for determining the environmental feasibility of a resource project, resource accounting should be used. This means that net benefits should be adjusted each year over the life of the project to allow for resource or environmental depletion.

Projects with differing environmental impacts

Many projects have few adverse environmental impacts and, hence, do not require EIAs. However, this must be determined by careful identification. For example, education or medical projects may be regarded as harmless to the environment until it is discovered that the buildings required are to be erected on wetlands, or that the chemical wastes from the laboratories are to be dumped in a river. There are some projects for which mitigation measures can be readily prescribed. These include agro-industries, crop intensification, fish farming, small-scale irrigation projects, water supply and sanitation, housing, and small-scale industries. It is important, however, that the mitigation measures be allowed for in the project design. Projects with significant adverse environmental impacts that impose severe mitigation problems include large-scale irrigation and water management, river basin development/drainage, new land development for agricultural and urban use, livestock, population resettlement, projects in forests and other environmentally sensitive areas, new airports, power generation, surface mining, and large industrial plants. For such projects some environmental damage is probably inevitable, but it is important to know the full costs to be able to compare the social costs with the social benefits.

Environmental Obligations of MDBs

In recent years MDBs and bilateral assistance agencies have assumed, or have been forced to assume, obligations relating to environmental impacts of the projects they finance that go well beyond their direct impacts. Roads financed by MDBs may have little direct impact on forests or other sensitive areas they traverse, but the migrants attracted by the roads may do extensive environmental damage. Plans for a multipurpose dam may provide for the mitigation of direct environmental impacts, but if the government does not carry out its obligations to resettle the families displaced by the reservoir, they may migrate to areas where they do considerable damage. Most of the environmental disasters in developing countries that MDBs are accused of financing are a consequence of indirect impacts. MDBs are, therefore, required to be responsible for a range of government activities associated with the projects they support. In the case of large projects, such as a billion dollar irrigation program or the Indonesian program for transferring hundreds of thousands of people from Java to the outer islands, MDBs must negotiate conditions in the loan agreement covering a wide range of government activities. For example, the government may be asked to compensate and resettle many thousands of displaced people in accordance with certain standards, or it may be asked to operate the irrigation system to prevent the overuse of water. In the case of projects that intrude on indigenous peoples, the government may be required to protect the culture of the natives, or to apply certain standards of equity in land transfers in the development of new communities. Countries receiving forestry loans may be required to adopt methods of harvesting and transporting timber that meet certain environmental standards, and to control migration into forested areas.

These new environmental obligations involve a range of planning and oversight activities by MDBs in their client countries never before contemplated. Negotiating loan agreements often involves MDBs in disputes between people of different regions or classes. For example, the World Bank's support of the Narmada River project in India (described in Chapter 6) has involved the Bank in a dispute between the poor villagers of the state of Madhya Pradesh who are destined to be displaced by the reservoir, and the more prosperous landowners and urban power users of the state of Gujarat who are alleged to benefit most from the project. The controversies associated with the social impacts of the dam have delayed Bank funding.

Conditionality in the form of environmental requirements is sometimes resented by governments of borrowing countries and may lead to disputes with the lender. For example, for political reasons the government may be motivated to locate a dam or a road or an agricultural program in a particular province, but the MDB may want it located elsewhere for environmental reasons. The MDB, of course, has the final word unless the borrower uses its political influence in the MDB to have the bank staff overruled. There is also a problem of credibility in loan conditionality, since many conditions agreed to by governments are for measures to be taken after the project is in operation. The MDB has no way of forcing clients to comply with its conditions once all the loan funds are paid out, but if the project turns out to be environmentally flawed or to cause social hardship, the MDB is often blamed because it financed the project. These are not hypothetical cases; they frequently occur.

A problem also arises when the environmental feasibility of the project or program involves the enactment or enforcement of laws and regulations that apply to a number of firms or activities in the country. A loan condition that an industrial plant treat its waste before dumping it into the river would not be very effective if dozens of other plants dumped untreated waste in the waterway. Therefore, the loan condition should be that the government inaugurate a program for controlling all sources of pollution in the rivers, including municipal and industrial sources. A loan to finance a hydroelectric facility to be located on a river in a tropical forest should be accompanied by conditions that protect the forest and the river, not only from direct environmental damage from construction and operation of the dam to the maximum degree possible, but also from the indirect impacts associated with the roads required to bring workers and materials to the dam site and to erect the transmission lines, and from the creation of a permanent community for the operators and their families. This type of conditionality involves development planning for a large area that might have been undisturbed in the absence of the hydroelectric facilities. Thus, in carrying out their environmental obligations, MDBs are participating in development planning and policy determination to a degree not contemplated a few years ago.

Nonproject Loans

Loans not tied to specific projects are a large component of MDB lending, and more than 50 percent of the loans made by the World Bank and IDA fall into this category. They take the form of industrial program loans providing financing for a number of private and government projects; loans to credit institutions that relend to small business and to farms; SALs made to governments to assist them in adjusting their economies to improve their balance of payments, or to eliminate fiscal deficits, or liberalize trade. Although the domestic relending agencies are supposed to follow environmental guidelines in making subloans, MDBs do not give attention to the individual projects. The SALs, which accounted for about 30 percent of World Bank and IDA lending in FY 1989, provide for conditions in the loan agreements dealing largely with macroeconomic policies, such as fiscal, monetary, and trade. As of 1991, specific undertakings on environmental protection or natural resource conservation had not been included in SAL conditionality. However, the World Bank is in the process of negotiating an environmental program loan with Turkey that would finance a range of pollution abatement and coastal restoration programs.

Some environmental economists believe that SALs should be accompanied by government commitments to enact and enforce pollution abatement measures, measures to protect tropical forests and watersheds, and programs to reduce soil erosion and degradation. In a recent article by two World Bank environmental economists, it was stated that 'The Bank is now convinced that the pervasive nature of environmental problems dictates a new approach: integrating environmental management into economic policy-making at all levels of government, supplementing the traditional project-by-project approach' (Warford and Partow, 1989). The article goes on to say that 'structural adjustment lending has not, until recently, paid specific attention to environmental issues. . . . Nevertheless, more explicit consideration of the effects of adjustment lending on the environment is necessary, not only to avoid possibly damaging environmental consequences, but also to fully use the potential of adjustment lending in improving environmental conditions.'

There is a strong argument for applying environmental and resource conditionality to SALs. Environmental degradation is often an important barrier to economic growth and to long-term balance of payments adjustment. Badly polluted cities reduce industrial productivity and discourage investment. Pollution reduces the availability of water for agricultural and industrial uses, and soil loss and degradation mean reduced farm output. SALs should provide for government commitments to four- or five-year environmental and resource management programs, with loan payments dependent upon performance. Such conditionality could be more effective in moving a country toward good environmental practice than tying environmental conditions to specific projects.

SALs should be used to induce and facilitate a change in the allocation of a nation's resources and in its investment priorities. Countries heavily dependent on a rapidly depleting mineral or on timber should be encouraged and assisted to shift to less resource-intensive production. In many cases, the remedy for structural disequilibrium is improved resource management. This usually means conserving resources that are being rapidly depleted, developing renewable resources such as forests, and shifting investment to labor- and capital-intensive industries. An unpublished study of the Tunisian economy found that dryland farming on marginal lands is destroying the productivity of areas formerly used for grazing, and that these activities have been fostered by rapid population growth that cannot find employment in areas with better soil. Such a development path is unsustainable because the erosion of the marginal land will eventually impair the fertility of the good land as well. Tunisian cities are overcrowded and highly polluted because of industrial activities and inadequate facilities for waste disposal. The conclusion of the study is that Tunisia should not try to expand agricultural production with labor working on marginal lands, but should favor industrial expansion in a number of smaller cities with production oriented to foreign markets. This recommendation illustrates the integration of development strategy with sustainability of resources.

To cite another example, Egypt is faced with a long-run shortage of water and, given the country's present water consumption pattern, available water will not meet demand by the year 2000. The water supply problem is exacerbated by pollution from agriculture, industry, and municipal waste, and water pollution limits the extent to which water can be recycled. The high rate of fertilizer use required to compensate for nutrients formerly supplied by silt now retained in the High Aswan Dam reservoir has caused a rapid growth of aquatic weeds in canals and drains. The weeds slow water flow in the canals, clog and deteriorate waterpumps, and increase water evaporation. An unpublished study recommends that Egypt abandon the objective of increasing land reclamation or expanding irrigated cotton production, and put greater emphasis on export-oriented industries. It also recommends that Egypt improve its water supply by reducing pollution of surface and groundwater, and use water more economically.

The above examples show how promotion of sustainability of the resource base, as opposed to short-term balance of payments adjustment, can deal with more fundamental adjustment problems. Broad shifts in a country's resource use and investment patterns could be promoted by conditionality applied to SALs and program loans for particular economic sectors.

IMF structural adjustment loans

Traditionally, the IMF has made intermediate-term loans to assist countries to restore balance of payments equilibrium, and these loans have been accompanied by conditions fostering equilibrium – usually changes in exchange rates and monetary and fiscal policies. Since the mid-1980s the IMF has been making longer maturity loans under its 'structural adjustment facility,' which serve much the same purposes as the World Bank's SALs. Conditionality associated with these loans has sometimes gone beyond the traditional to include measures for promoting exports and freeing trade and investment. Environmental organizations have been recommending that the IMF as well as the MDBs include a requirement in its loan conditionality that borrowers adopt environmental policies. Although the IMF staff has tended to reject this recommendation, pressure has been brought by the US Congress to incorporate the environment into its operational and policy objectives. The 1990 Foreign Operations Appropriations Bill (HR 2491) requests the Secretary of the Treasury to recommend: (a) the addition of environmental and natural resource specialists to the Fund's staff; (b) a systematic process taking into account the impact of IMF lending activities on the environment, public health, and poverty; and (c) the creation of lending terms to promote sustainable management of natural resources and measures that would reduce external debt in exchange for domestic investment in conservation and environmental management. Although it is not expected that the IMF will tie its loans to the enactment of specific pollution abatement laws or resource conservation measures, it would be desirable to include progress in protecting the environment and improving resource management in its general conditionality. Since the IMF and World Bank frequently collaborate when both are making structural adjustment loans to the same member country, IMF credits might be made available to support the environmental programs specified in World Bank SALs. In this way, IMF conditionality could be tied to environmental and resource management programs specified in the World Bank loans.

The Allocation of Capital in Developing Countries

Development assistance agencies are in a strategic position to influence the allocation of capital investment in Third World countries. This is true even though their loans represent a small percentage of total investment in these countries. Only a fraction of the payment for projects supported by MDBs is financed by the loan; the remainder comes from domestic sources or external loans from private sources, often facilitated by the MDB loans. In addition, the projects themselves require or induce large complementary investments. For example, loans for power generation and transmission may induce investments in power-intensive industries, and loans for urban development and industry may have multiple effects on investments in industrial metropolitan centers. Loans for highways and railroads influence the regional allocation of the total capital resources of a nation. MDBs need to consider whether their own portfolios are influencing the total allocation of a nation's capital resources in a way that promotes sustainable development. MDBs can also influence government capital outlays by the conditionality associated with their nonproject loans.

The issue of how a nation's capital, and government expenditure generally, should be directed toward promoting sustainable development is highly complex and differs greatly between developing countries. There is, however, a consensus among environmental economists that many poor countries do not devote enough resources to social programs, to improving the productivity of the rural sector, and to promoting small, private enterprise. These areas are increasingly believed to constitute the basic sources of long-run development. The 1991 OECD *Report on Development Cooperation* (DAC) gives special emphasis to the growing potential of micro-enterprises and to 'participatory developments,' which are programs in which the masses participate in selecting, financing, and administering through community-based organizations and small private enterprises. To quote from a recent OECD publication:

> The debt crisis of the 1980s revealed the many weaknesses of development strategies which depend upon large-scale state intervention in the economy and ushered in a new era in thinking that gives far more importance to the activities and decisions of the private sector. More recently, the donor community has focused attention on devising aid strategies and projects that draw people more directly into economic, social, and political life. These two fundamental shifts in orientation can be addressed simultaneously through measures that support the development of micro-enterprises. (Halvorson-Quevedo, 1991/2, p. 7)

The 1991 DAC report stresses participatory development in programs for education, training, and health; for selecting, designing, and implementing aid-financed projects through community-based organizations; and for supporting micro-enterprise (Love, 1991/2, p. 5). Some examples of external assistance to micro-enterprises and to programs administered by NGOs are given in Chapter 7.

It is easy to recommend that MDBs shift more of their loans and technical assistance to small enterprises in rural communities, to community-based NGOs for initiating and administering social programs, and to agricultural research, training, and extension services in which the farmers themselves participate. But how can these institutions that were organized to make large loans to governments conduct business with thousands or millions of NGOs and small private firms? They can only do so by operating through governmental or large private institutions that have close relations with community-based NGOs and small private enterprises. In most countries, the nonpolitical institutional framework for administering these programs does not exist, and this framework cannot evolve in an environment of central government dictatorship or in the absence of democracy and political and social equality. Moreover, since the MDBs must receive the interest and principal payments on their loans in foreign exchange, they must look to the central government for servicing the loans, and central governments are reluctant to guarantee loans to entities they do not control. MDBs have affiliates that are permitted to make loans without government guarantees, but these institutions loan mainly to large private domestic and foreign enterprises. Bilateral agencies, such as USAID and its counterparts in other industrial countries and a number of private foundations, are in a better position to channel loans to NGOs than are the MDBs and their affiliates, but the MDBs have the bulk of the available development assistance resources. If there is to be a substantial change in the direction of MDB lending along the lines indicated in the 1991 DAC Report, it may be necessary either to create new forms of multilateral development assistance or to make radical changes in the existing organizations.

Global Environmental Facility (GEF)

Developing countries are important agents in activities that affect the quality of the global environment, the most critical of which are:

1   Protection of the ozone layer.
2   Limitation of greenhouse gases in the atmosphere.
3   Protection of oceans and their aquatic life.
4   Protection of biodiversity.

The global environment is a multinational commons. Its quality is of vital interest to all countries, but unilateral measures to protect or improve it provide little benefit for individual countries. International agreements on joint actions are necessary to achieve goals in terms of damage limitation, but where significant national costs are involved, there has been an international consensus that the costs to developing countries should be subsidized at least in part by the developed countries. In November 1990 twenty-five developed and developing nations agreed to establish a GEF to be administered jointly by the World Bank, the United Nations Development Programme (UNDP), and the United Nations Environmental Programme (UNEP). Other nations are expected to join, with developed countries contributing to a fund of about $1.5 billion for a three-year pilot program. The GEF is designed to help finance programs and projects affecting the global environment that would normally not be funded by loans from MDBs, thus providing the developing country participants with an additional source of international capital. Such loans are available for countries with a 1989 per capita GDP of $4000 or less.

Loans are to be made available on concessional terms (lower interest rates than those normally provided by the MDBs).

Summary

Over the past decade, especially since 1990 when MDBs began requiring ElAs for all supported projects involving environmental problems, the environment has become an important part of the agenda for foreign assistance agencies. However, much remains to be done. The EIA process needs to pay more attention to the sustainability criteria and the procedures for approving projects for support require more definitive guidelines to assure compatibility of projects and programs with sustainable development. Also, environmental conditionality should be extended to SALs. Finally, greater attention needs to be given to the allocation of capital among economic sectors and between rural and urban regions for promoting sustainable development goals.

The brief case studies in Chapter 6 illustrate some of the ways in which MDBs have failed to apply environmental standards to their lending programs in the past, while the case studies in Chapter 7 illustrate projects that embody sound environmental and resource conservation principles.

NOTES

1 The Harrod–Domar model, the basic elements of which were developed independently by two economists (Harrod, 1948; Domar, 1946) was a byproduct of the Keynesian revolution in income and employment theory. Both authors were concerned with the rate of growth that would just maintain full employment over time. This critical rate of growth was shown to depend upon the relationship between income and spending, on the one hand, and the additional output generated by an additional volume of investment, on the other. The additional income or output, dY_t, is a function of the incremental capital–output ratio, *ICOR*, and the initial volume of investment, I_t. Assuming saving and investment are equal, we have $I_t = sY_t$ at full employment, where s is the ratio of savings, S_t, to income, Y_t. Hence, the rate of growth, g, may be expressed as

$$\frac{I_t/Y_t}{ICOR}$$

or the ratio of the investment coefficient to the incremental capital–output ratio. *ICOR* is a constant at any time point, but changes over time with technological progress.

2 The World Bank charges rates of interest on its loans that are comparable to its own cost of borrowing in the international capital markets, plus a margin for administration and reserve. World Bank obligations are guaranteed by member countries.

3   The IFC is an affiliate of the Bank that makes loans to private domestic and foreign firms operating in developing countries. Unlike regular World Bank loans, these loans do not require the government guarantee of a member country.

4   An EIA is the investigation undertaken as the basis for an EIS, which is usually a summary of the findings of the investigation.

5   PL 101–240 Section 521 (December 1989) directed the Secretary of the Treasury to instruct the US executive directors for each MDB 'not to vote in favor of any action proposed to be taken by the respective bank which would have a significant effect on human environment, unless for at least 120 days before the date of the vote (a) an assessment analyzing the environmental impacts of the proposed action and of alternatives to the proposed action has been completed by the borrowing country or the institution, and been made available to the board of directors of the institution; and (b) . . . such assessment or a comprehensive summary of such assessment has been made available by the MDB to effective groups and local nongovernmental organizations.' The Act further states that the US executive directors are to initiate discussions and propose procedures 'for the systematic environmental assessment of development projects for which the respective bank provides financial assistance, taking into consideration the guidelines and principles for environmental impact assessment promulgated by the United Nations Environmental Programme and other bilateral or multilateral assessment procedures.'

REFERENCES

Domar, Evsey D. (1946) Capital expansion, rate of growth and employment. *Econometrica*, **14** (April), 137–47.

Harrod, Roy F. (1948) *Towards a Dynamic Economics*. London: Macmillan.

Halvorson-Quevedo, Ruandi (1991/2) The growing potential of micro-enterprises. *OECD Observer*, December/January.

Love, Alexander R. (Chair of DAC) (1991/2) Participatory development and democracy. *OECD Observer*, December/January.

United Nations (1951) *Measures for the Economic Development of Underdeveloped Countries* (report by a group of experts appointed by the Secretary General). New York: United Nations.

UNESCAP (1985) *Environmental Impact Assessment: Guidelines for Planners and Decision Makers*. Bangkok: UN Economic and Social Commission for Asia and the Pacific.

Warford, Jeremy and Partow, Z. (1989) Evolution of the World Bank's environmental policy. *Finance and Development*, December, 5–8.

6

Case Studies on Environmental and Resource Management Problems in Development Projects and Programs

Introduction

The interest in Third World development on the part of environmentalists arose in considerable measure from case studies of environmental disasters that took the form of the destruction of tropical forests, the pollution of lakes and rivers once enjoyed by tourists, the destruction of the cultures of 'primitive' people, and the killing of wildlife to the point of extinction. Much of this concern reflects the fears of people in industrial countries about the harm being done to the global environment, including the loss of biodiversity, and about the loss of wildlife and beautiful scenery that they enjoy visiting and remembering. Only a few environmentalists are deeply concerned with the destruction of the resource base in Third World countries and its implications for sustainable development. Since multilateral development banks (MDBs) have financed many of the environmentally flawed development projects, environmentalists have tended to blame them for the tragedies. Some environmentalists believe that foreign aid has done much more harm than good, but there is no evidence that developing countries are not capable of generating just as much ecological damage without external help.

The short case studies in this chapter illustrate violations of sound environmental and resource management principles in some development projects and programs. The failures noted in these projects are not unique, and hundreds of environmentally flawed projects have been found. They are not presented to give the reader the impression that all development projects supported by MDBs are environmentally flawed. MDB officials learn from past mistakes and, given the recent adoption of EIAs as a condition for supporting projects, responsible governments and external assistance agencies will be sponsoring more successful projects in the future. Mention should also be made of the fact that many development projects that reveal serious environmental shortcomings may still contribute to an increase in net social welfare and even to sustainable development. Therefore, the criticisms of the projects reviewed in this chapter do not necessarily imply that they should not have been undertaken. The shortcomings do suggest that the projects could have contributed more to sustainable development had the environmental and natural resource deficiencies been avoided or mitigated.

The Narmada River Irrigation and Power Projects

The Narmada River projects in India together constitute the largest single irrigation and power program in the world, involving 30 major dams, 135 medium dams, and 3000 small dams – all to be built over the next 50 years on the Narmada River and its tributaries. The first phase of the plan is to build the Sardar Sarovar Dam in the state of Gujarat, which is designed to serve an irrigation area of about 1.9 million hectares, and to provide 1200 megawatts (MW) of power. The project, which was supported by a World Bank loan of $450 million in 1985, was only 10 percent completed in mid-1990. A second multipurpose dam for which World Bank Group financing has been requested, the Narmada Sagar project, would irrigate an area of about 141,000 ha and generate 1000 MW of power. The reservoir for the Sardar Sarovar project would require displacement and resettlement of an estimated 70,000 people, while in the case of the Narmada Sargar project some 80,000 people will have to be resettled. Taken together the two projects will flood some 43,000 ha of cultivated land, and some 51,000 ha of forestland, much of it already denuded. The total cost of the Sardar Sarovar dam project alone (excluding the irrigation and drainage costs) is estimated at $1.9 billion, of which the foreign exchange cost is $630 million.

These projects have given rise to substantial opposition, both within India and among conservation organizations in the industrial countries. The major concerns have been: the resettlement of those displaced by the dams; the distribution of the benefits and costs between the rich and poor in the country; the destruction of forests and wildlife; and the environmental impacts on the land and on the water basin. Also, doubts have been expressed regarding the economic feasibility of the project.

The major elements of the Sardar Sarovar project include: (a) the dam and power generating facilities; (b) power transmission lines; (c) resettlement and rehabilitation of those displaced by the reservoir; (d) the irrigation system and drainage facilities; and (e) roads and other infrastructure. The major benefit affecting the largest population would be from the irrigation of some two million hectares to be occupied by 340,000 households. Irrigation would raise cropping intensities by more than 100 percent by replacing rainfed crops. Food crops, including rice, sorghum, and wheat, are projected to increase by over 300 percent and cash crops, including mustard, groundnuts, and cotton, by 270 percent (Searle, 1987a, pp. 8–17).

Intensive cultivation in the project area is estimated to provide 0.7 million man years of additional employment, most of which would benefit landless laborers. Net farm income is projected to increase by 484 percent. The project would provide a substantial increase in the volume of water supplied to urban and rural centers, and the total installed power generating capacity planned for the complex is 1450 MW, with most of the power going for industrial and urban use. There would also be an increase in fisheries by the creation of the reservoir, but this might be partially offset by damage to existing fishing downstream. Finally, there will be some benefit from flood moderation, but this is not a major objective.

Environmental effects

No comprehensive EIA for the Sardar Sarovar project was conducted before the World Bank loan was made in 1985 and a number of environmental studies still have not been completed. The major impacts arise from flooding 37,000 ha for the reservoir – of which 18 percent is forested, 33 percent is cultivatable land, and about 50 percent has low utilization potential. Wildlife will be affected, but escape corridors are to be maintained during the filling of the reservoir. Large reservoir and canal systems frequently create health problems from malaria, filaria, schistosomiasis, and other water-related diseases. It is believed that these diseases can be controlled. The major environmental problems have to do with the forced displacement of 70,000 to 90,000 tribal and rural poor people. The Sardar Sarovar reservoir would affect approximately 248 villages in three Indian states – Maharashtra, Gujarat, and Madhya Pradesh. Resettlement must take place in accordance with the rules for involuntary settlement established by the World Bank as a condition for funding. These rules, which are supposed to be in line with those adopted and implemented by the Narmada Control Authority and the Disputes Tribunal, are as follows:

(1) Every family which loses more than 25 percent of its landholdings must be allocated an irrigatable plot of the same size with a minimum of 2 ha and a maximum as allowed by land ceiling laws. Irrigation facilities must be provided by the state in whose territory the allotted land falls. Resettled landholders must be compensated for the land they lose and are to be charged for the land they acquire at a price to be fixed by the states. The initial payment to be made for the new purchase is 50 percent of the compensation they receive and the balance is to be paid off over 20 years, interest free.

(2) All persons displaced, including the landless who are mostly tribal, are to regain at least their previous standard of living after a reasonable transition period and to be economically and socially integrated into the new community.

(3) People are to be relocated as village units, village sections, or families in accordance with their preference; fully integrated in the community in which they are resettled; and provided with appropriate compensation, and adequate social rehabilitation and physical infrastructure, including community services and facilities. Landless displaced persons are entitled to a stable means of livelihood in either the agricultural or nonagricultural sectors.

(4) Displaced people who have historically made their living from the forest and its products may be moved on to lands controlled by the Indian Forest Conservation Act. However, deforestation should be kept at a minimum.

Criticisms

Criticisms of the Narmada River Program are of two general types. First, there are criticisms of particular environmental impacts, such as impacts on forests, wildlife, and tribal societies, and the socioeconomic impact on the oustees, even if they are given all they have been promised. Many critics of particular environmental and social impacts of the program would prefer to see the scheme abandoned entirely. However, most of the environmental impacts, and some of the socioeconomic impacts as well, can be moderated or compensated for. Clearly, the Bank has an obligation to deal with these issues in terms of its own guidelines before releasing the remainder of the loan funds or making new loans. (In 1991 the Bank had under consideration a $150 million IDA loan for watershed development in the Sardar Sarovar project area, including fishery development, management and preservation of wildlife sanctuaries, and Narmada River basin planning.)

A second type of criticism is that the entire project is flawed because the total economic benefits (whether discounted or not) are less than the total monetary costs plus the nonmonetary social costs, including the adverse environmental impacts on the land, the forest, the river basin, and the people that are displaced. This criticism is difficult to evaluate since there has not been a comprehensive social benefit–cost accounting for either the entire Narmada River program or any of its components by either opponents or supporters. Nor, to my knowledge, have the critics presented detailed alternatives for providing the expansion of irrigated land that India will require for its agricultural needs.

Much of the general opposition to the project is based on a generic criticism of large multipurpose dams. Although this criticism tends to be anecdotal, a significant number of large irrigation programs have failed to live up to their expectations in terms of the increased productivity of the land. Because of poor management and lack of training of the farmers, salinization and waterlogging have resulted in low yields and in some cases the soil has not been appropriate for the type of irrigation provided. Yet there is impressive evidence that irrigation has greatly enhanced farm yield, and dependence on rainfed farming alone would have made impossible the current level of agricultural output in India and other Third World countries. What are lacking are specific proposals for alternative irrigation systems that would increase net social benefits.

One of the criticisms made against the Bank loan for Sardar Sarovar is the failure of either the Bank or the Indian state governments to review the energy alternatives to the hydropower portion of the project. Energy specialists have provided impressive evidence on how conservation in India could reduce the need for new hydropower capacity. Other critics have pointed to several uncompleted irrigation projects to which investment funds might have been directed instead of to an entirely new large project. Critics have also pointed out that the Tawa Dam, completed in the mid-1970s (also on the Narmada River), irrigated only 87,000 ha in contrast to an expected potential of 332,000 ha, and that the cost of the dam increased 232 percent over the initial estimate.[1] An objective evaluation of the Narmada project has been complicated by political conflict and demonstrations by Indian opponents to the project, largely related to the resettlement plan and the relative benefits and costs to the inhabitants of the different Indian states affected. The charge is made that the rich receive most of the benefits while the poor bear the costs.

The above criticisms led to an extensive Bank review and a delay in further Bank assistance. Because of the criticisms, on May 22, 1990 the Japanese Ministry of Foreign Affairs decided to halt additional funding for the Narmada Sarovar project. Some of the problems might have been avoided had there been a comprehensive EIA of the project before the Bank's initial loan in 1985. However, given the size, number, and diversity of the populations affected by the project, many of the political and social problems raised would probably have continued. India is not an easy country to assist.

The Cameroon Forestry Project

Cameroon is a West African country with low population density, over half of which is covered by tropical rainforest. The forest is home to a Pygmy population of about 50,000 and to numerous elephants, forest buffalo, and gorillas. The Cameroon forestry project, which is being financed by a $30 million World Bank loan, is a good example of the environmental problems associated with the management of tropical forests, and of the conflicts between generating revenue from the forests on the one hand, and applying conservation principles to tropical forest management on the other.

The 1990 Cameroon forestry plan was based on recommendations by the United Nations Food and Agricultural Organization (UNFAO) and the UNDP, under the framework of the Tropical Forest Action Plan (TFAP).[2] A major part of the Cameroon TFAP is to open up a large forested area in the south and southeast of the country through a 600-kilometer road and Atlantic port, with the road leading from the coastal town of Kribi to the town of Yokadoumo, deep in the southeast area. Logs are to be produced mainly for the world export market, providing foreign exchange and creating 100,000 jobs over a 20-year period. In Cameroon, logging is carried on under concessions held by international logging companies (mostly French, Dutch, and German). According to the Cameroon TFAP, government-financed infrastructure will hold down transportation and other costs. There are also fiscal incentives, such as reduced taxes and duties to encourage investment in logging.[3]

Of the $136 million in total investment in the project over a period of five years, 38 percent is to go for institutions (including a training center for foresters, a research institute, and government organizations responsible for reforestation, soil conservation, and plantation development). The plan calls for 27 percent of the total investment to be devoted to forest-based industries, including mills, 23 percent to forestry and land use, 9 percent to forest conservation, and 3 percent to fuelwood production.

Criticisms

The major criticism of the Cameroon forestry project by environmentalists is that it puts too much emphasis on commercial logging for the export market, and gives insufficient attention to natural resource conservation, the provision of fuelwood, and the impact of logging on indigenous people. The major interest of the Cameroon government is to exploit the forests for export income, which the country greatly needs because of its large external debt and its projected decline in foreign exchange earnings from petroleum. Therefore, any forestry program acceptable to the government must have a large commercial logging and export component. This objective could very well rule out logging consistent with sustainability, such as selective logging and minimum use of roads to avoid damage by the logging process. A reforestation program might permit sustainability of timber production, but not be environmentally sustainable.

Another criticism of the program is that there is little involvement of the local communities, indigenous peoples, or NGOs, either in planning or in operation. The original TFAP philosophy stressed support and participation by village communities and NGOs, but there seems to be little recognition of this in the forest management program. The only role for the people living in the forest will be that a few of them will serve as laborers for the timber companies. Moreover, the issue of land tenure and community land rights has been ignored, for both the rural farming community and the large population of semi-nomadic Pygmies. The latter live mainly in the largely untouched dense tropical forests, and the project will have an impact on the natural forest ecosystems that sustain their traditional way of life.

Critics also charge that the program devotes inadequate attention to fuelwood, which is the major source of energy. They argue that the plan lacks a rational fuelwood production program, including agro-forestry and on-farm forestry for fuelwood production, together with facilities for marketing and distribution. This could generate substantial income for the rural population.

A further criticism of the Cameroon forestry program is that insufficient attention is paid to conservation and reforestation directed toward sustained yield management. It is estimated that about 200,000 ha is being deforested each year through agricultural encroachment alone, but this problem is not addressed. In addition, little is being done to reduce the current inefficiency of forest harvesting. The vast bulk of commercial timber harvest utilizes only three of the 30 timber species in the forests, and 30–40 percent of each tree is wasted when felled. The species not harvested are harmed by the selective logging practices and there is further waste during wood processing.

The rate of deforestation in the Cameroon dense tropical forests is estimated at ten to eleven times the rate of regeneration, and the country's forest stock is threatened with exhaustion within a few decades. The Cameroon TFAP proposes to bring 200,000 ha per year under sustained yield management out of a total of some 22 million hectares in the forested areas. Thus, relatively little provision is made for reforestation compared with the extent of the new rainforest areas opened to logging – an area of some 14 million hectares.

Finally, doubts are expressed regarding the economic justification of the program in terms of net revenues generated, after taking into account government expenditures and fiscal incentives, such as tax reductions. A full accounting of the net social benefits would need to include a monetary valuation of the social, environmental, and resource costs of the increased deforestation. Moreover, public expenditures of $136 million spent on alternative projects might create more than the 100,000 jobs estimated for the forestry program. Attention might have been paid to agro-forestry and making better use of animals and plants in the forest ecosystems. Such projects could be environmentally sustainable and would enhance the welfare of the people living in and near the forest areas.

The Brazilian Northwest Region Development Program (Polonoroeste)[4]

Frontier areas, whether they consist of forests or unoccupied marginal lands, have always been looked upon as potential development areas that can provide larger output and private land ownership for landless populations. A number of Latin American countries have sought to realize these objectives in their huge tropical forest frontiers. The Brazilian Polonoroeste Program provided for the settlement of 30,000 families in the states of Rondonia and Mato Grosso. During 1981–5 these migrants were in addition to the existing new settlement population in the area, most of which had arrived during the previous decade. The new settlers were to engage in agriculture, cattle raising, and timber production. The initial federal government budget for the program was $1.1 billion, of which 57 percent was for roads to provide access to the area and most of the remainder was for settlement infrastructure and community services, such as education, health, and communications. The World Bank agreed to provide over $400 million to support the program. The projects to be financed included: the paving of road BR 364 and the building of connecting feeder roads ($240 million); agricultural development and environmental protection ($67 million); health ($13 million); new settlements in unoccupied areas of Rondonia ($65 million); and a rural development project in the Mato Grosso ($26 million).

Much of the project area in the Mato Grosso had been settled for ten to twenty years. In addition to providing for the new settlers, the program was designed to provide agricultural and social services to all settlers by establishing rural community centers, improving physical infrastructure (including roads and crop storage), and providing social services. Much of the area for new settlement in Rondonia was unoccupied land, mainly publicly owned tropical forests where productive activities comprised rubber tapping, mineral prospecting, and extractive forest operations. The project was to provide new immigrants with land facilities and assistance for up to 15,000 families by 1989, to provide infrastructure and services, and to develop forestry operations and tree crops suited to the Amazon environment. Settlers would produce subsistence crops, commercial food crops, and export crops, such as rubber and coffee. In the longer term, they were to become involved in forestry.

Each settler family was allotted a 100 ha plot, half of which was to be kept in a legal forest reserve. Timber recovery was to be promoted by the establishment of sawmills, and it was intended that sustained forestry operations would be undertaken on 525,000 ha of legal forest reserves. A principal benefit of the project was to be rubber, and plantation production was expected to replace wild rubber tapping, which at that time accounted for 80 percent of domestic production. Some coffee was to be planted, but the area allotted for coffee had poor soil. Livestock and fruit constituted the other important products.

The number of migrants increased rapidly, both selected families and a large number of spontaneous migrants. In some areas forest clearing occurred at a very rapid rate, often more for tree cropping and land speculation than for agriculture.

The World Bank loan agreement specified a number of environmental and social conditions. These included regulations on forest clearance, monitoring and control of incursions by migrants into forest reserve areas, awarding of land to selected farm migrant families, and protection of the Amerindians.

Criticisms

Perhaps no development program supported by MDBs has been criticized as harshly and as broadly as the Polonoroeste Program. World attention was drawn to the large-scale destruction of tropical forests and its implication for global warming. Actually, the Polonoroeste program was responsible for somewhat less deforestation than the rapid growth of the livestock industry in the Amazon outside the program. Cattle ranching was supported by Brazilian government development agencies, one of the most important of which was the Superintendencia do Desenvolvimento da Amazonia (SUDAM). SUDAM provided tax-based subsidies to cattle ranchers and industrial wood producers in the Amazon (Browder, 1988, pp. 247–97).

The Polonoroeste Program brought widespread criticism to both the government of Brazil and the World Bank. In addition to the deforestation, the government and the Bank were criticized for the poor quality of the soil in the settlement areas, the lack of skills of the migrants, poor planning and supervision of the settlement program, the failure to keep out or provide for the large number of unsolicited migrants who were attracted by the Bank-financed paving of the 1500 kilometer highway BR 364, and the failure to protect the land reserves, environment, and health of the indigenous indians.

These problems arose in part because loan agreements between the World Bank and the Brazilian government for dealing with migrants and protecting Amerindians were not adhered to by the government. In 1985 the Bank imposed a temporary halt on disbursements of the undistributed balance of the loan, pending additional guarantees by the Brazilian government that the rights of the tribal people in Rondonia would be respected. This is one of the few cases in which World Bank officials admitted to errors in their loan programs. In a public speech, Bank President Barber Conable characterized Polonoroeste as a 'sobering example of an environmentally sound effort which went wrong. The Bank misread the human, institutional, and physical realities of the jungle and the frontier. . . . Protective measures to shelter fragile and tribal people were included; they were not, however, carefully timed or adequately monitored' (Conable, 1987).

In 1990 the World Bank had under consideration a $167 million loan to Brazil for the Rondonia Natural Resources Management Project, which is designed to deal with some of the environmental impacts of the Polonoroeste Program. It provides for, among other things, forest management support, environmental and tribal protection, and support for small farmer community projects and social services. However, major conservation organizations in the USA find serious flaws in the new loan project. These findings were set forth in a letter to E. Patrick Coady, US Executive Director of the World Bank, accompanied by a detailed memorandum on the principal findings and recommendations of the organizations. The memorandum made the following points (Environmental Defense Fund, 1990b):

(1) The Bank should insist that the Brazilian authorities legally regularize the Amerindian Reserves and protected natural areas whose legal regularization and protection were a condition of the 1981–3 Polonoroeste loans.

(2) NGOs, local unions, and indigenous and community groups in Rondonia maintain that, contrary to Bank claims, there has been little or no substantive consultation with, or participation of, groups representing the target populations and beneficiaries of the project: Amerindians, rubber tappers, and agricultural colonists. The Bank should ensure that representatives of the Amerindians, rubber tappers, and small farmers are given full access to information on the project and participate in its planning. More than recipients of most Bank loans, this project is being justified on its prospective environmental and social benefits to these peoples. Therefore, their active involvement and participation are indispensable.

(3) Disbursements should be linked to a schedule to establish 17 Amerindian reserves and four protected natural areas that should have been established under the first Polonoroeste project. Of particular concern is the situation in the Guapore Biological Reserve, whose establishment was a specific condition of the 1981 Polonoroeste loan. The reserve has not been protected from illegal logging, land speculation, illegal colonization, and mining encroachments.

(4) Loan disbursements should be linked to the establishment of the physical integrity of the other agro-ecological zones. For example, areas designed as agro-ecological zones are suffering from ongoing road construction, government-endorsed land claims, illegal logging, land speculation, and forest clearing.

(5) Although the project acknowledges that access to credit for smallholder agriculturalists is absolutely essential for success, its agricultural credit component is gravely flawed and inadequate. It should be reformulated to include smallholder cultivation of perennial crops.

(6) Greater attention needs to be given to the environmental and

health problems caused by gold mining along the Madeira River and its tributaries. Studies indicate that the entire food chain of the Madeira is showing signs of toxic contamination from the gold mining activities. There is little analysis of gold mining's impacts on the project area, and effective measures have not been proposed to address these impacts.

Consideration of the World Bank loan for the Rondonia Natural Resource Management project was suspended in 1991 and will not be considered again until 1992.

Resettlement of Persons Displaced by the Manantali Dam in Mali

The Manantali Dam on the Senegal River, which was completed in 1988, was designed for the following objectives: (a) irrigation of 375,000 ha; (b) river navigation throughout the year from the mouth of the river to Kayes, giving land-locked Mali direct access to the sea; and (c) annual generation of an average of 800 gigawatt-hours of energy. The cost of the dam and other parts of the program was estimated at more than $800 million, to be financed by Arab and European donors, the AfDB, the Canadian government, and the UNDP. USAID agreed to fund the Manantali resettlement for approximately $18 million. The impoundment reservoir for the dam forced the removal of about 10,000 people from 31 villages, the largest of which had 900 inhabitants and the average about 350.

A survey and analysis of the resettlement program was undertaken by Koenig and Horowitz (1988), supported by Clark University and the Institute for Development Anthropology, and funded by USAID. This case study is based on that survey.

The original resettlement plan called for the creation of 11 new villages, all but one of which were to be substantially larger than former villages. However, field studies done for USAID and the Mali government found that most people opposed being agglomerated with other villagers in the new settlements. Hence, plans were made for 34 new village sites. Before resettlement, the people lived in one of the most isolated areas of Mali, with an overall population density of less than five per square kilometer. Their economy was a combination of subsistence and some commercial production, including dryland agriculture and livestock.

The resettlement area, which is directly downstream from the dam, is sparsely populated. Although the soils appear to be fertile and the rainfall adequate, one reason for the sparse settlement is the presence of tropical diseases, such as schistosomiasis, malaria, and onchocerciasis (river blindness). However, a control program for the diseases was instituted by the World Health Organization. The group preparing the survey of the resettlement program suggested that the areas were not as attractive as those from which at least some of the people were displaced. Before displacement, the villagers supplemented agriculture and herding by hunting and foraging. The authors of the survey believe that the resettlement area contains less useful fauna and flora.

The managers of the resettlement project concentrated on the construction of new villages, provision of infrastructure, and clearing of land in the new sites. The project did not include a development program involving the introduction of new economic activities. The basic objective was replacement of existing resources, including the availability of land and water. All the new villages were provided with boreholes and hand pumps for water, and cisterns to store water during times when pumps were inoperable. The new villages are some distance from the river since the riverine lands are reserved for an irrigation scheme. The benefits from the dam – irrigation, navigation and hydropower – will accrue to areas far downstream, outside the settlement area.

Criticisms

In assessing the resettlement project, the survey report considered three questions: (a) Are the resources in the resettlement area adequate for the reestablishment of the prior standard of living? (b) What opportunities do the relocated populations have for directing the resettlement process to their own advantage? (c) What kind of development infrastructure has been put in place to facilitate sustainable and equitable economic growth?

The major criticism of the resettlement project by the authors of the survey is that planning did not take sufficient account of what people would produce to earn a living. 'Resettlement was seen more as the technical problem of rebuilding, rather than as the process of maintaining and improving the standard of living' (Koenig and Horowitz, 1988, p. 12). For example, attention was not given to the opportunities provided by the new settlement area for fishing or for new agricultural activities. The resettlement area is quite isolated and must have trade and other economic associations with the region and the country. Yet consideration was not given to what the area might specialize in to export, what it would need to import, and how a trade balance might be achieved. Finally, the people resettled should have been given a greater opportunity to participate in both planning and decision making during the construction period. For example, people should have been given more responsibility for building their own homes, including the choice of either building them themselves or having them built.

Indonesian Transmigration Program

Resource-oriented development, which dominated economic development policy throughout most of the past two centuries, has favored the migration of people in high population density areas to frontier areas with low population density and abundant land and forest resources. These migrations have frequently been unsuccessful or the development fruits have occurred two or three generations after they were initiated. Even in the USA, including my home state of Oregon, there are large areas of abandoned farms and towns, relics of nineteenth-century migrations that failed at great human and environmental cost. Some of the reasons for the failures are illustrated by the Indonesian Transmigration Program (ITMP). Whether this gigantic movement will eventually prove to be a net social gain or loss remains to be seen.

Large migrations promoted by governments may fail for several reasons. First, the land and the resources are often incompatible with the type of economic activities planned or with the skills and experience of the migrants. Frequently, the land is of marginal quality, which is often the reason the area was not settled generations before. This is especially true of tropical rain-forests, which tend to have poor soils for agricultural crops. Considerable experimentation is necessary to determine the best uses for frontier areas. This takes place with minimum social cost with gradual migration, but can be very costly for a large settlement. A second reason is the absence of infrastructure in new communities; there is not sufficient economic surplus from a new venture to create the infrastructure. Rapidly constructed roads, utilities, hospitals, power facilities, schools and homes, financed by external subsidies, are likely to be costly, inefficient, and inappropriate for actual requirements.

A third reason is the isolation of the new communities. New settlement areas require strong links with the remainder of the country to provide materials, services, and markets, and these links are usually inadequate by reason of distance and poor communication facilities. Another reason is that migrant families are often poorly selected for a frontier environment, and workers lack skills and experience for new economic activities that often require considerable innovation and experimentation. Finally, there is likely to be considerable environmental damage as the need for survival promotes quick returns from resource exploitation and little incentive for conservation. For all these reasons, the social costs of large migrations are often very high and the social benefits small in comparison with other development strategies. The motivation for these programs is often political, since they provide an alternative to satisfying demands for land ownership and employment through land reform and better utilization of resources in the already settled areas of the country.

The ITMP actually began in colonial times, but was not launched on a large scale until 1969. Since then more than two million people have been resettled in the outer islands of Sumatra, Kalimantan, Sulawesi, and Irian Jaya, with the migrants recruited from densely populated rural areas of Java, Medura, Bali, and Lombok. The Indonesian government views the program 'as a means for providing the landless and other rural poor of the Inner Islands with land assets which offer the opportunity over time for productive labor and increasing income' (Searle, 1987a, p. 118). Since its first loan for the program in 1976, the World Bank has been continuously involved, and as of 1986 had committed over half a billion dollars to financing transmigration and swamp reclamation, plus technical and financial support for smallholders, some of whom were indigenous people. In 1986 the Bank imposed a temporary moratorium on releasing payments under earlier loans because of the serious environmental and social problems created by the program. At the time of writing, the Bank had under consideration an additional loan of $140 million for the ITMP.

The ITMP has experienced virtually all the problems outlined above. Evaluation of the program is difficult because of large differences between the performance evaluation of the Indonesian government and the World Bank on the one hand, and Indonesian and foreign critics of the program on the other.[5] There have been a number of phases in the total program covering different periods and involving different outer islands, and the experience has not been uniform. The World Bank's overall assessment has been favorable in terms of food production and family income, but yields were lower than projected and land was not put into food crop production on the scale expected (World Bank, 1988, pp. 161–2). External critics have charged that some of the settlements have been disastrous failures and some settlers are worse off than they were before resettlement. There has been severe criticism of the settlements on wetlands, and one report states that neither the crops (mainly rice) nor the settlers were suited to the soil and other conditions in the settlement area (NDRC, 1990, p. 13).

Much of the criticism of the ITMP concerns the destruction of tropical forests and the treatment of the indigenous population in Irian Jaya, where people have been forcibly resettled and subjected to various pressures from migrants, in some cases causing them to flee across the border to Papua New Guinea. It is charged that most of the Bank's guidelines for the treatment of indigenous people have been violated by the ITMP (*Ecologist*, 1986, p. 60). It is also charged that too much resettlement has been on tropical forest areas with poor soils for farming. Finally, it is argued that by improving watershed management, increasing irrigation, and controlling siltation on the island of Java from which many of the migrants came, food production could have been increased on already farmed land at a far lower economic and environmental cost than on the outer islands (*Ecologist*, 1986, p. 171). However, there are no data available to the present author to support this contention.

The Ok Tedi Mine in Papua New Guinea

The Ok Tedi mine in Papua New Guinea (PNG) is located in a mountainous region with a sparse population consisting of indigenous people whose livelihood is heavily dependent upon the tropical forests and rivers where they dwell.[6] The Ok Tedi copper and gold deposit is geographically and geologically similar to a nearby mine on the Indonesian side of the island of New Guinea, the Ertsberg mine, built by an American company, Freeport Indonesia. However, the Ertsberg mine has experienced fewer problems arising from the disturbance of the indigenous people in the area.

The Ok Tedi mine is 80 percent owned by a consortium consisting of BHP Minerals (Australian), Amoco Minerals (US), and a group of German firms, and 20 percent owned by the PNG government. The mine is on Mount Fubilan in the Star mountains of northeastern PNG. The entire mountain is to be mined to its base. It originally consisted of copper oxide ore with a gold-bearing cap. The gold is leached with cyanide and the copper is processed to concentrates. The area has extremely heavy rainfall, severe seismic activity, and unstable geology. Two rivers, the Fly and the Ok Tedi, are near the base of the mountain and the indigenous people depend heavily on fish and other aquatic life from the rivers along which their villages are situated. They practice subsistence agriculture using riverbank gardens vulnerable to flooding, which can be exacerbated by the sediment deposited from the mine into the rivers. Metals, chemicals, and other substances discharged into the rivers impair water quality for consumption and kill the fish.

During negotiations with the PNG government for a concession agreement that provided for exploration and the preparation of a feasibility study prior to the submission of a proposal for a mining agreement, the Ok Tedi consortium undertook to prepare an EIA as part of the feasibility study, but insisted on a budgetary ceiling of $180,000. The cost of an adequate EIA would have run far higher, but the consortium refused to make additional expenditures until it had an agreement to build the mine. Before the approval of the mining agreement in 1980, there was a dispute between the consortium and the government, which had undertaken an environmental investigation of its own. There was disagreement regarding how much waste rock would be allowed to be dumped into the river and whether the cyanide used in the gold extraction should be neutralized. Also at issue were environmental monitoring and compensation for injury or damage arising from the environmental impacts of the project. Agreement was reached on a maximum limit of 60 million tonnes of waste rock to be dumped into the river, and on the construction of facilities to neutralize the cyanide, but neither of these arrangements was satisfactorily completed. The tailings disposal system fell behind construction schedule and was abandoned when a massive landslide dumped some 50 million tonnes of waste into the center of the dam site. To get the mine operating without a waste disposal dam, the PNG government agreed to let the Ok Tedi consortium try a temporary method of chemically neutralizing the waste before the tailings were released into the rivers. However, there were two accidental releases of untreated cyanide into the rivers and villagers found dead fish, and even a dead crocodile, floating in the water. In February 1985, the government ordered the mine to be shut down, but later, fearing that because of low copper prices the company would mine the gold cap and then withdraw without proceeding to mine the copper ore, it allowed the mine to reopen under an agreement that the company would build a permanent tailings waste dam. However, completion of the dam was delayed by construction and financial difficulties and the company was allowed to release untreated tailings into the rivers. The native population lodged serious complaints regarding the reduced fish catch in the Fly river and actually tried to bar the company from shipping on the river.

In 1989 the PNG government was again faced with the option of shutting down the mine or allowing continued disposal of tailings and waste rock into the river system. However, shutting down the mine would have meant a loss to the government of $35 million in 1990, and an $860 million loss for the remainder of the life of the mine. The decision was made especially difficult because the Bougainville copper mine, also 20 percent owned by the PNG government, was forced to close in that same year because of civil disturbances. (The local population was critical of the environmental damage done by the mine on the island of Bougainville and demanded independence from PNG.) Again, the PNG Cabinet decided in favor of the mine.

This case study illustrates the problems that developing countries may have in requiring mining companies to conduct adequate EIAs before negotiation of mining agreements. In this case, an adequate EIA might have cost $25–30 million, but would have indicated the problems to be faced in mining Mount Fubilan in an environmentally sound manner, given the conditions of geologic instability and heavy rainfall. Not only was the company unwilling to undertake such an outlay without the assurance of a mining agreement, but it might not have been willing to commit itself to all the environmental mitigation expenditures recommended by the EIA. Perhaps the government should have had the courage to shut down the mine rather than allowing the company to continue operations under the environmentally unsatisfactory conditions, but it was heavily dependent upon the prospective income from the mine for its development programs.

The Carajas Iron Ore Project in Brazil

The Carajas iron ore project is an example of inadequate environmental planning on the part of both the World Bank, which helped finance the project, and the Brazilian government, which sponsored the Greater Carajas Program (GCP) of which the iron ore project is a part.[7] This massive regional program, covering nearly 900,000 square miles of eastern Amazonia, includes iron ore, copper, bauxite, tin, and gold mining; pig iron and aluminum production; semi-manufactured steel products; cattle ranching; agriculture; logging; a large railroad complex; and several new towns with several hundred thousand migrants. Total investment in the project will be well over $60 billion. This project in the states of Pará and Maranhão has been directly and indirectly responsible for the widespread destruction of the tropical forests and a social upheaval of the Amerindians.

In 1982, the World Bank loaned $304 million to the Brazilian state mining company, Valle do Rio Doce (CVRD), for the construction of the Carajas iron ore mine and a 490 kilometer railroad to transport ore to a port on the Amazon. The Bank also assisted CVRD in raising external capital, totaling $3.6 billion, from both public and private sources. Some of the ore was scheduled to be processed into pig iron in smelters located along the railroad. A confidential World Bank staff appraisal report (1982) made a detailed examination of the technical and financial aspects of the project, but except for arrangements for protection of the health, safety, and land rights of the Amerindians, there was virtually no discussion of environmental impacts and no attempt to estimate the cost of the loss of the tropical forests and other resource damage in calculating the rate of return on the project. The estimated financial rate of return of 11 percent was actually less than the Bank's normal minimum internal rate of return of 12 percent. Considering the natural resource loss involved and the technical and market risks of the project, this rate of return appears to be quite low.

Missing from the staff appraisal was the plan to produce pig iron from the ore with fuel to be derived from charcoal produced from native forests. The Greater Carajas council has approved 22 charcoal-fired pig iron smelters, four of which were in operation by 1989, and all of which use native forests for fuel. The trees used for making charcoal are supposed to be replanted and available for future charcoal production, but there is considerable doubt whether suitable (replanted) trees will grow in the area. The smelters are not included in the iron ore project financed by the Bank, but CVRD has helped to finance and promote the smelters, and they were part of the GCP plan before the Bank loan was negotiated.

The loan agreement with the Bank provided that the iron ore company be responsible for protecting the 10,000 Amerindians in the region and also required measures to protect the environment within the project area, defined as a 100 kilometer radius around the mine and railroad. It is reported that the program for the Amerindians has been inadequate, that their lands have been invaded by illegal logging and mining, and that the promised legal demarcation of the Indian areas to protect their territorial and cultural rights has not been implemented (Bank Information Center, 1989). The 22 planned pig iron smelters, which are partially owned by CVRD, threaten both air and river quality, and a large area of tropical forest. This portion of the project should have been canceled, but the Bank has reportedly denied any responsibility for the smelters. Since all the funds loaned for the project were disbursed by 1986, it is now powerless to act.

NOTES

1 For a discussion of criticisms of the Narmada Sarovar project, see Udall (1990).
2 The TFAP is a set of guidelines and a broad financing plan launched in 1985 by the FAO, the World Bank, UNDP, and the World Resources Institute (WRI) in response to the rapid pace of tropical forest destruction. A number of developed and developing countries and the major external assistance agencies are involved in the TFAP. Currently the TFAP is managed by the FAO, but there has been considerable dissatisfaction with the TFAP and it is under review.
3 Most of the material for this case study is taken from Searle (1987b, pp. 58–91). Some of the criticisms of the project are based on the Environmental Defense Fund (1990a).
4 Information for this case study is derived from the Environmental Defense Fund (1990b).
5 For a criticism of the program see *Ecologist* (1986) and Natural Resource Defense Council and the Indonesian Environmental Forum (1990). For a World Bank assessment see World Bank (1988).
6 Material for this case study has been largely derived from Pintz (1987) and Mikesell (1983, Chapter 13).
7 Information for this case study was derived in part from Bank Information Center (1989).

REFERENCES

Bank Information Center (1989) Carajas iron ore/greater Carajas project. *Funding Ecological and Social Destruction: The World Bank and International Monetary Fund*. Washington, DC: World Bank.

Browder, John O. (1988) Public policy and deforestation of the Brazilian Amazon. In R. Repetto and M. Gillis (eds), *Public Policies and the Misuse of Forest Resources*. New York: Cambridge University Press for World Resources Institute.

Conable, Barber B. (1987) Speech before World Resources Institute. Washington, DC: World Bank, May 5.

Ecologist (1986) Indonesia's transmigration programme: a special report in collaboration with Survival International and TAPOL. *Ecologist*, 16(2/3).

Environmental Defense Fund (1990a). *Case Study of the TFAP for the West African Nation of the Cameroons* (mimeo). Washington, DC: Environmental Defense Fund.

Environmental Defense Fund (1990b) Letter to E. Patrick Coady, and
   memorandum entitled Issues that need to be addressed and resolved in the
   Rondonia natural resources management project (mimeo). Washington, DC:
   Environmental Defense Fund, January 9.
Koenig, Delores and Horowitz, Michael M. (1988) *Lessons of Manantali: A
   Preliminary Assessment of Involuntary Relocation in Mali*. Binghampton, NY:
   Institute for Development Anthropology.
Mikesell, Raymond F. (1983) *Foreign Investment in Mining Projects*. Cambridge,
   MA: Oelgeschlager, Gunn and Hain.
Natural Resource Defense Council and Indonesian Environmental Forum (1990)
   *Bogged Down: The Tragic Legacy of the World Bank and Wetlands
   Transmigration in Indonesia*. Washington, DC: National Resources Defense
   Council.
Pintz, William S. (1987) Environmental negotiations in the Ok Tedi mine in
   Papua New Guinea. In C. Pearson (ed.), *Multinational Corporations*. Durham,
   NC: Duke University Press for World Resources Institute.
Searle, Graham (1987a) *Indonesian Transmigration in Major World Bank
   Projects*. Wadebridge, Cornwall: Wadebridge Ecological Centre.
Searle, Graham (1987b) The Polonoroeste Project. In *Major World Bank
   Projects: Their Impact on People, Society and the Environment*. Wadebridge,
   Cornwall: Wadebridge Ecological Centre.
Udall, Lori (1990) Statement on behalf of the Environmental Defense Fund and
   other conservation organizations before the Subcommittee on International
   Economic Policy, Trade, Oceans and Environment, Committee on Foreign
   Relations, US Senate. Washington, DC: Environmental Defense Fund, July 18.
World Bank (1988) *Indonesia: The Transmigration Programme in Perspective*
   (Country Study). Washington, DC: World Bank.

7

Positive Programs for Sustainable Development

Introduction

Sustainable development economists have been critical of the way development lending institutions have allocated their loan capital between the urban–industrial and the rural sectors, between projects for expanding physical output and those for social services such as education and health, and between large capital-intensive projects that benefit only a small portion of the population and small projects designed to increase the productivity of small farms and industrial enterprises. They see a greater need to provide feeder roads for thousands of small villages than to build four-lane highways between large cities, or to pipe clean water to rural communities than to supply cheap power for urban homes and office buildings.

Environmental economists do not see more foreign aid as it has been provided and managed in the past as a solution to the current or long-term problems of developing countries. They believe that in many countries foreign assistance programs have been oriented to maintaining an affluent and high energy-consuming urban economy enjoyed by the bureaucracy, the military, and the professional and rentier classes, while two-thirds of the population live in poverty without access to education and health facilities. Also, as the *World Development Report 1991* points out, a large portion of foreign capital finances additional consumption rather than productive investment. Capital flight has been very high, in some countries exceeding official development assistance and borrowing from private foreign sources.

Sustainable development economists would revolutionize the current approach to development and external assistance by shifting the emphasis from physical capital formation to the conservation and productivity of natural resources and human capital investment. They favor small projects designed to increase agricultural productivity, to halt soil loss and degradation, to promote small industrial operations, and to promote education and training. This approach involves large technical service and education components and substantial participation by the mass of the people the programs are designed to help. It would replace state control and private monopoly with community-based administration and small private enterprise. It is oriented to giving a large portion of the population secure tenure to the land they occupy, freedom to produce and market in accordance with economic incentives, and the knowledge and ability to make rational choices.

A major problem for economic development is how to create a dynamic small enterprise sector that would mobilize the skills and savings of a large segment of the economy, particularly outside metropolitan centers. This objective is being promoted by a growing number of programs designed to assist small enterprises similar to those illustrated in this chapter. A strong small business sector is lacking in most developing countries, and industrial activity is dominated by government enterprise and large private firms that often receive substantial assistance from the government.

According to environmental economists, generous official economic assistance and the availability of loans from private international markets have not only been ineffective in promoting development, but have been counterproductive in three ways. First, many of the large capital-intensive projects that foreign aid has supported have been environmentally flawed and destructive of natural resources. Second, aid often enables countries to postpone improvements in macroeconomic management and the mobilization of domestic resources. Third, private and public external loans have increased indebtedness beyond the capacity of the borrowers to make service payments, with the result that future foreign financing for highly productive projects has been jeopardized. Moreover, efforts to maintain debt service payments have often been at the expense of social services.

An adequate program of human development cannot be launched in many developing countries without a political and social revolution that will provide opportunities for participation by the masses in a modern productive social and economic system. This social revolution should release the enormous productive power of women from the bondage of limited education and economic repression, in the absence of which half the population is constrained from realizing its potential contribution. In many countries, this constraint also applies to religious and ethnic minorities. It is ironic that in some countries female members of the elite class can become heads of state while the majority of women are chattels. External development agencies are limited in their ability to bring about the political and social changes necessary for sustainable development. However, they could make a contribution by supporting more projects in which there is participation and administration by the people who work in and are benefited by the project.

The three major MDBs all maintain small enterprise loan and technical assistance programs, but in the past these programs have tended to be administered by government-controlled intermediaries. The MDBs are just beginning to provide some assistance through nonprofit NGOs, cooperatives owned by small and cottage-industry manufacturers, and farmers. USAID, European bilateral aid agencies, and the UNDP have been more successful in stimulating small enterprise. Several of these projects are illustrated in the brief case studies of successful development described in the following sections.

Project Agro Forestier (PAF) in Burkina Faso

Most of the funds for agricultural projects provided by multinational development banks go to support large multipurpose dams and irrigation projects that create the environmental and social problems illustrated in Chapter 6. Some of them can be justified, but in many cases the social benefits are not high enough to warrant the gigantic costs. In recent years, many of the most successful agricultural projects in terms of increased yields and contributions to sustainable development have been small, low-technology projects in which poor farmers themselves play an important role. The Burkina Faso PAF is such a project.[1]

This project, which was funded and managed by Oxfam, a private development organization, was organized and designed to prevent soil erosion and increase crop yield through water conservation. The Yatenga region of Burkina Faso where the project is located has a history of overuse of land resources and decreasing arable land surface caused by severe erosion. The PAF developed a simple, inexpensive, labor-intensive technology for collecting water and holding it in the fields, thereby increasing the land's absorption of water and preventing erosion. An agriculture extension service was established to teach farmers about the technology, which is now used on thousands of farms. An important feature of the project has been the participation of local farmers in the development of the technology, which has evolved through the experimentation of those using it.

The PAF began operation in 1979 and the techniques first introduced were those developed in the arid regions of Israel. Low earth walls were used to enclose one square meter of land, called a 'microcatchment,' in which a basin was dug to collect water from the surface. Initially trees and later various crops were planted in the squares. Later on, rocks were used for the walls enclosing the squares because the earthen ones tended to be washed out by heavy rains and required continuous repair.

The system works to improve crop yields in two ways: (a) it bounds rainwater on the fields rather than letting it run off, thereby increasing the absorption of water by the land; and (b) the fertilizer (usually manure) and organic materials applied to the fields are less likely to be washed away. These are the short-run advantages. Over the longer run this technology facilitates erosion control and improves soil quality. Soil accumulates behind the barriers and promotes the growth of crops where previously only bushes and trees could grow. The results show an average increase in yield of 67 percent on the test plots using the technique, with the highest yield differentials occurring in years with low rainfall. The latter enhances the contribution of the technique by helping to prevent malnutrition or starvation in years of drought. The internal rate of return to the PAF project on the staff and materials investment has been estimated at 37–42 percent.

Much of the success of the PAF program is attributed to the extension service for bringing the technology to the farmers. Communication between agricultural research and the extension service has been facilitated because the researchers are also extension agents, and all research has been carried out on the farms in the region, with participation by the farmers in the experimental stages of the project. The fact that the project is low-tech, low-cost and low-risk has also contributed to its success, compared with capital-intensive projects designed and executed largely by expatriates using modern equipment. Thousands of farmers now use the technique and the number continues to grow as people observe its success.

Renewing Niger's Soil

Like most other countries in Sahelian Africa, Niger has experienced abnormally low rainfall during much of the past 30 years. The population has been increasing at 3 percent per year, while food production has been increasing at only 1 percent per annum; up to one-third of the population faces a chronic food shortage. By cultivation of marginal land, the area under crops has doubled over the past 20 years, but grain yield per hectare has declined by one-third. Assuming that the chronic drought continues, and in the absence of a large-scale irrigation program, Niger's food problem might be considered hopeless. But this is not the conclusion of agricultural specialists who have been conducting experiments in Burkina Faso, Mali, and Niger.

In 1981 a Sahelian branch of the International Crops Research Institute for the Semi-Arid Tropics (ICRISAT) was established with the objective of transferring Asia's 'Green Revolution' to Africa's semi-arid tropics.[2] ICRISAT was founded by the Ford and Rockefeller Foundations and is funded by more than 30 agencies, including UNDP. In the early 1980s, the Institute tested improved varieties of grain throughout the Sahelian region, but the seeds produced no better yields than local seeds. They found that while the lack of rain is a major obstacle to increasing output, the real problem is the lack of soil fertility. Specifically, they found that the soil contains too little phosphorus and nitrogen, but with the addition of these nutrients the local varieties achieved a threefold increase in yield. Nitrogen can be provided with nitrogen-fixing legumes such as cowpeas, while the phosphates have to be imported. After the legumes are harvested, the stalks make good animal fodder, and the animals tend to avoid grazing on grains planted in combination with legumes. Improved farming methods can also stop wind erosion, improve fertility, and reduce damage from pests. ICRISAT agro-foresters studied the use of various grasses and shrubs as wind barriers and found the indigenous gamba grass and a shrub, *Acacia bauhinia*, to be useful for sheltering crops. Scientists are optimistic that if farmers are persuaded to adopt these techniques, Niger and its neighboring countries can greatly lessen their dependence on food imports.

Because Niger lacks foreign exchange, a problem arises in importing the 30,000 tonnes per year of phosphate that Niger requires. However, a recent study funded by the European Community and USAID found that sufficient phosphates could be supplied by exploiting phosphate deposits in Niger. These phosphates have not been used because they are not soluble. However, the study proposed a process using sulphuric acid to make them soluble. It is suggested that if Niger's phosphate reserves – estimated at more than one billion tonnes – were developed, the country might be able to produce enough phosphate beyond its own needs for export. In this way Niger could earn some of the capital required to tap deep underground water reserves for irrigation. This project provides an example of how a research-oriented project with a relatively modest budget can make a substantial contribution to sustainable development.

Three Biosphere Reserves in Central America

The Sian Ka'an Reserve in Mexico

Wildlife and ecological reserves are important for preserving world biodiversity and should be established throughout the world to protect the wildlife and the ecosystem peculiar to each of hundreds of unique areas. A problem often arises in how to deal with the local people living in the area and with other natives who may have been visiting the area to hunt and fish for many generations. This problem was encountered in the establishment of the Sian Ka'an Biosphere Reserve in the Yucatan Peninsula of Mexico in 1986.[3] The area contains 528,000 ha of tropical moist forest, marshes, mangrove swamps, and freshwater and marine ecosystems containing 1200 species of vascular plants, 320 species of birds, and seven species of endangered vertebrates. Before the establishment of the reserve by the Mexican government, the area was in danger of being used for slash and burn agriculture and cattle ranching. Sian Ka'an consists of a 'central core zone' and a buffer zone devoted to small-scale farming, lobster fishing, and coconut growing. The Secretariat for Urban Development and Ecology is responsible for Reserve management and it designates a board composed of federal, state, and municipal officials. A council of representatives composed of local residents, scientists, and public officials was created to provide a forum for discussion for planning and a channel for direct involvement with the reserve management.

In addition to the research projects conducted within the reserve, a private nonprofit organization conducts research on the residents' economic activities. This organization, called Amigos de Sian Ka'an, receives funding from the World Wildlife Fund and the Nature Conservancy, while the research projects conducted within the reserve are financed primarily by the Mexican government. In addition to lobster research and inducements to the fishermen to use sustainable fishing methods, research has been conducted on a disease affecting the region's coconut palms. Amigos de Sian Ka'an has also established a model farm to demonstrate sustainable methods of intensive farming. About one-fifth of the residents are involved directly or indirectly in the reserve, primarily through participation in reserve projects. The major reason for the project's success has been the involvement of local residents, and the creation of the reserve has enhanced rather than impaired their incomes. Sian Ka'an is part of an international network of biosphere reserves established by the United Nations Educational, Scientific and Cultural Organization (UNESCO). There are 269 such reserves in 70 countries, two-thirds of which are in developing countries.

The Maya Biosphere Reserve in Guatemala

In early 1990 the Guatemalan government established the 1.4 million hectare Maya Biosphere Reserve in the Petén district of northern Guatemala.[4] This action saved from destruction a rich tropical forest area containing Tikal (the ancient capital of the Mayan civilization) and a number of ecological riches, including the threatened black howler monkey. The Maya Reserve adjoins the Calakmul Biosphere Reserve across the Mexican border in the Yucatan, which was established at about the same time. The Nature Conservancy played an important role in surveying and establishing the reserve's boundaries and recommending preservation of the area to the Guatemalan government. Without this action the area would have been subjected to slash and burn agriculture and uncontrolled hunting. USAID assisted in the conservation program and has made a contribution to Guatemala's National Protected Areas Council for supporting management activities at the Reserve (Houseal, 1990, pp. 16–21).

The Kuna Biosphere Comarca

The Kuna Biosphere Comarca is a natural reserve established by the Kuna Indian Tribe on their reservation on the Caribbean coast of Panama, over which the Kuna have sovereign rights.[5] In the mid-1980s a 150,000 ha area was established by the General Kuna Congress with a core area of 60,000 ha, which is to be part of the UNESCO Biosphere Reserve network. The Kuna established the reserve because they believed a branch of the Pan-American highway being built into the area would bring an influx of migrants that would destroy the forest and probably engage in cattle ranching.

Pakistan's New Silk Industry

Since ancient times, when the camel caravans journeyed from China to the Mediterranean, Pakistan has obtained its silk from China at an estimated annual foreign exchange cost of $4.5 million. The Pakistan Forest Institute (PFI), with assistance from the UNDP and the UNFAO, developed new lines of indigenous silkworms and mulberry bushes on which they feed.[6] Efforts are also being made to train Pakistanis for the silk industry, which PFI hopes will eventually generate employment for 15,000 families. Silk production is a labor-intensive industry which can be carried out in the home at all stages, and could provide occupation for women in the rural areas, who by custom almost never leave the home.

Considerable research and experimentation was required to develop pure lines of silkworms, which must be bred through many generations to achieve stability in producing the desired silk characteristics. Since the silkworm must be killed before the silk can be extracted, production is limited by the availability of eggs produced by crossing lines of locally evolved parent stock. Raw silk comes from cocoons that have been dried in a machine for up to six hours at appropriate temperatures. It requires nine kilograms of fresh or green cocoons to produce one kilogram of raw silk, and on one hectare of mulberry bushes a farmer can raise enough silkworms to produce 750 kilograms of green cocoons a year, which will yield a profit of $900. Continuous experimentation is ongoing to improve the quality of the silk, the efficiency of the process, and the leaf yield of the mulberry bushes.

Before the project, locally produced silk met only 20 percent of Pakistan's annual demand of 750 tons of yarn. To expand production, UNDP has established two silkworm breeding facilities which also serve as distribution outlets for the silkworms. Since the project began in 1984 more than 200 farmers have been trained and in 1990 over a million mulberry bush cuttings were distributed to private farmers. Loans and subsidies for farmers interested in sericulture are made available by PFI.

If PFI's hopes of expanding sericulture to the point at which the country could become self-sufficient in silk production are to be realized, it will be necessary to train and employ civil servants to take over the operation of the project when the foreign experts depart. It will also be necessary to attract large numbers of families and private firms into the various stages of the industry. Thus far the government has not assigned a sufficiently high priority to the promotion of the industry.

Flood Control Project in Tanzania

Before completion of the flood control project in the Great Rift Valley of Tanzania, the residents of Mto wa Mbu township lived in fear of finding their homes and farms submerged in floodwaters from three rivers.[7] Beginning in 1975, the people of the area asked government officials for help in building flood control drains to guide water coming from the steep hills into the three local rivers, constructing intake canals to transfer the overflow water to the main irrigation canal, and draining the swamplands which were a breeding ground for malaria-carrying mosquitoes. The government obtained technical assistance and financial support from the UNDP. A team of irrigation engineers, project managers, and economists was assembled with the help of the International Labour Organization (ILO), and area residents provided the labor, some offering part of their services without pay. Twenty-five years after the completion of the project Mto wa Mbu's production of bananas, maize, rice, cassava, and coconut had increased by nearly 50 percent and average farmer income rose fourfold, as a result of being able to grow crops on land reclaimed from swamps and the absence of the destructive annual flooding.

This project is part of a larger UNDP-supported public works program in Tanzania, which includes improvement of water supply, flood control, irrigation, rural access roads, and housing construction, to which the UNDP has contributed $6 million since 1979. In the words of a former UNDP resident representative, 'a "small is beautiful approach" works. The project is proving that low-cost methods for constructing and maintaining an irrigation system can promote self reliance and create income' (Hart, 1989, p. 26). This self-help approach was based on the principle that an entire community gains when villagers contribute to a project's success.

Combining Forest Reserves with Irrigation Projects in Indonesia

The Dumoga Valley on Sulawesi island is an area of 30,000 ha of fertile land that was subjected to rapid development in the 1970s and to substantial immigration under the government-sponsored transmigration program.[8] There was concern for protecting the tropical rainforest in the area, which is essential to maintaining water resources in Dumoga and is also a very rich ecosystem. In 1977 the World Wildlife Fund (WWF) and the Indonesian Nature Conservation Department (PPA) proposed that the government establish a nature reserve that would include catchment areas of the Dumoga headwaters, which are vital to the region's water supply and planned irrigation projects in the valley. At the same time, the World Bank was investigating a proposal for loans to finance the Kosinggolan and Toruat irrigation projects. Before initiation of these projects, a team from the WWF and the PPA identified the tropical rainforests of Dumoga as very rich in species and proposed establishment of a nature reserve there. The government agreed to the proposal for the Dumoga reserve, together with a reserve on the Bone and Bulawa rivers. A World Bank appraisal team expressed concern about the need for water catchment protection, and the local government agreed to cancel forest concessions to halt cutting on the headwaters of the rivers. This was made a condition for the Bank loan following proposals by the WWF. By 1980 three reserves formed a continuous area of about 300,000 ha and it was proposed that they become a national park.

This is a good example of cooperation between an environmental organization, which investigated the environmental and development importance of a forest reserve, and the World Bank, which made disbursement of the loan dependent on forest protection to guarantee sufficient water flows to the irrigation area. The two projects were completed by 1987 and the Dumoga-Bone National Park was established in the same year. All development objectives were accomplished and the irrigation schemes boosted rice production and helped convert the province from a rice-importing to a rice-exporting region.

'Protected Agriculture' in Egypt

'Protected agriculture' is a labor-intensive means of producing horticulture crops in tropical countries on a year-round basis.[9] Vegetables, fruits, and flowers can be produced under plastic greenhouses for export and domestic use with one-third the water required for open-field cultivation, and with yields up to sevenfold higher. Pest and disease control are also far easier in greenhouses. Egypt is well suited to 'protected agriculture,' but training, extension service, and research are necessary to expand the industry. These services are provided by the Dokki Research and Training Centre in Cairo, which was assisted by a $1.3 million grant from UNDP and technical support from FAO. Since its inception in 1988, the Dokki Centre has trained 800 specialists and carries on experiments to improve the technology of production in plastic greenhouses, using carefully controlled amounts of water and fertilizer.

Courses at the Dokki Centre are offered free of charge and many of the trainees, of whom at least one-third are women, have graduated from agricultural colleges. Other trainees are practicing farmers. The government has been offering five acres (two hectares) of land in newly reclaimed desert areas and a greenhouse to qualified applicants. The center also offers specialized courses using computers for climate control, irrigation, plant nutrition, and pest management, and supports extension teams that have been teaching techniques to some 3000 producers.

Egypt began practicing commercial 'protected' cultivation with imported greenhouse structures in the mid-1980s and by 1990 there were several domestic factories producing materials for greenhouses. Thousands of greenhouses have been put into operation and two-thirds are privately owned. The UNDP has supported the Plastic Development Center for Agricultural Purposes, which produces materials for greenhouses. Given Egypt's potential water shortage and abundant labor, horticultural commodities produced in greenhouses are an ideal industry for expanding the country's national income. The program is environmentally benign and less costly than reclaiming desert land for an equivalent amount of open-field crop production.

Horticulture Commodities in Kenya

Horticulture commodities, including fruits, vegetables, and cut flowers, are a rapidly expanding source of export income for African and Latin American countries and provide an important supplement to earnings from crops with slow-growing markets, such as coffee, cocoa, cotton, and tea. Production is labor-intensive and well suited to small enterprise operating with only one or two hectares. The industry was initiated on a small scale in Kenya in the 1950s, but expanded very rapidly during the 1970s, with substantial assistance from the government beginning in 1968.[10] Early in the industry's history large-scale private farmers established contacts with European marketing firms and, in some cases, foreign investors provided financing, often as partners in joint ventures. Most of the small farmers rely on export agents to collect the produce and arrange for its transport and sale abroad. The volume of exports rose from 1476 tonnes in 1968 to 36,200 tonnes in 1986, and in that year accounted for over 3 percent of the value of Kenya's exports.

Unlike some African governments, which control prices to producers and maintain a monopoly on exports, the Kenyan government organization, the Horticultural Crops Development Authority (HCDA), has left prices largely in the hands of the private market and allowed market incentives to operate. The principal functions of the HCDA are to regulate exports, allocate air cargo space, and standardize containers. The HCDA also established packing stations for smallholders, developed a market information system, and provided production and market research. Direct government assistance has been small, but it has financed infrastructure for the industry. The government program has been limited to assisting an industry created and operated by private incentive and initiative. There have also been a number of projects relating to horticulture financed by bilateral assistance, mainly from European countries. These projects have included horticultural research, agricultural training, and irrigation.

Despite the contribution to Kenya's export earnings, the bulk of the horticulture produced is consumed locally, and the fruits and vegetables have become an increasing part of the Kenyan diet. The study from which this information has been drawn concluded that 'Without this combination of government assistance and government restraint, it is highly unlikely that the expansion in horticultural exports would have been as rapid or as large' (Shapiro and Wainaina, 1989, p. 18).

The Environmental Programme for the Mediterranean

The Mediterranean, on whose shores Western civilization arose, is becoming so seriously degraded that many of its beaches are not fit to swim from, its fish and seafood are dying, and its shoreline is loaded with pollution.[11] This is not caused simply by people throwing garbage into the sea, but by the poor environmental practices of the countries bordering the Mediterranean. Because of the interaction between land and sea, saving the Mediterranean from biological death requires an environmental revolution in the countries on its borders. The major sources of marine pollution are summarized as follows:

1 The discharge of untreated or partially treated organic wastes into rivers, estuaries, and the sea.
2 Agricultural runoff containing fertilizers, pesticides, and detergents discharged into waterbodies connected to the sea.
3 The discharge of industrial chemicals, including heavy metals, into the waterways.
4 The leakage of petroleum from ships and shore facilities into waterways.
5 Dumping of litter, including plastics and organic materials, on the shores by tourists, local residents, fishermen, and ships.
6 The siltation of waterways reaching the sea from agricultural fields and deforested hillsides, and from mine tailings and metal-rich soils.

These pollutants have a variety of effects on human health, aquatic life, economic efficiency, and coastal amenities. They contribute to human diseases, such as typhoid, eye and skin infections, polio, cholera, and hepatitis. They not only kill marine life but create health hazards for human consumers of fish and seafood. Siltation of lagoons and coastal waters destroys wetlands in the lagoons and deltas, reducing fish and bird populations. The discharge of phosphates and nitrates from agricultural runoff leads to the eutrophication of lagoons, bays, and gulfs, which results in excessive growth of algae, red and green tides, and fouling of beaches.

Because it is not possible to separate the activities having an adverse environmental impact on the sea and the coast from those that degrade air, water, and soil in the inland regions, environmental reform must encompass the entire area of the bordering countries. Environmental degradation is especially acute in the countries on the southern and eastern Mediterranean. The Environmental Programme for the Mediterranean (EPM) is targeted to entire countries not simply to the coastal areas.

The EPM was designed by the World Bank and the European Investment Bank (EIB) as a strategy for supporting environmental measures integrated with economic development in the Mediterranean countries (World Bank and EIB, 1980, p. 60). Under the EPM the two banks will promote the following objectives:

1 Encourage the development, preparation, and implementation of environmentally sound investment strategies at the country level.
2 Insure compatibility between environmental programs and economic development and support efforts to integrate environmental concerns into the mainstream of economic and social policy.
3 Encourage the adoption of policy measures conducive to an efficient use of natural resources.

The EPM has three closely linked parts: (a) a Multi-year Mediterranean Environmental Technical Assistance Program (METAP) launched in January 1990, funded by the two banks, the UNDP, and the European Community; (b) financing new environmental projects; and (c) integration of resources from other multilateral and bilateral donors to support METAP and EPM investment activities. The first phase of the program seeks to identify priority areas and types of actions; the second phase will prepare investment projects, determine institution-strengthening activities and define specific policy measures; and the third phase will implement these measures, projects, and activities. The report on which this case study is based constitutes the first of the EPM's three phases (World Bank and EIB, 1990). Although the report emphasizes the regional nature of the EPM, there appear to be few multinational projects, nor do most of the measures lend themselves to projects involving more than one country. The regional aspects of the program lie mainly in the mobilization of resources to be directed to the region, and the overall identification of necessary planning, data gathering, and monitoring related to the effects of the program on the Mediterranean region as a whole. One important area of coordination would be the adoption of uniform standards for pollution control by all countries involved, since there are important externalities arising from the common benefits of cleaning up the Mediterranean. Unfortunately, measures for achieving uniform standards and regulations were not discussed in the report.

The principal categories of environmental measures receiving the highest priority for EPM support are as follows:

1   Water resource management, including both surface and groundwater
    resources; the conservation and protection of water resources, such as
    incentives for water saving and recycling.
2   Management of solid hazardous waste, including identification of high-risk
    hazardous waste disposal sites and the enforcement of disposal standards;
    incentives for adopting low-waste technologies and recycling; and the
    adoption of the 'polluter pays' principle to both public and private sector
    sources of waste.
3   Avoidance of marine pollution from oils and chemicals, including prevention
    of spills, disaster preparedness, avoiding shipping accidents involving
    technical materials, and training personnel for dealing with emergencies.
4   Coastal zone management, including planning coastal area development, and
    protecting geologically sensitive coastal areas, especially wetlands, and
    habitats of migratory species.
5   Conservation of cultural heritage sites.

The METAP will pursue these objectives by working with the governments to develop a pipeline of environmental projects, to formulate and
improve environmental policies and regulations, and to strengthen the
governmental framework. The METAP will finance the feasibility studies
of projects and the carrying out of policy studies. It will make specific
recommendations for improving environmental legislative and regulatory
activities.

Economic policies, development strategies, and sustainable development

The EPM is more than a program to protect and restore the environment of
the Mediterranean basin. Despite its environmental and resource management orientation, the EPM must be regarded as a set of economic policy
recommendations and development strategies appropriate for both individual countries and the region. If it were nothing more than a list of recommended pollution abatement measures and of projects for pollution
mitigation to be supported by external assistance, it could not achieve its
environmental and resource management goals. The policies and investments for achieving these goals cannot be separated from the whole range
of national economic policies and the development strategies that determine
investment priorities. In other words, environmental objectives must be
fully integrated with development objectives and national economic
policies. Although the EPM Report reflects this integration, the authors fail
to make the point explicitly and to illustrate it with specific examples.

In contrast to the approach that makes economic development the center-
piece and environmental protection 'a subsidiary objective,' the EPM's
approach is unique in making sustainable development, with its environmental and natural resource management components, the single comprehensive objective. We may cite a few examples from the EPM Report
itself. The Report makes clear that pricing policies and subsidies may

increase the generation of pollution and mismanagement of natural resources. Some of the governments of the Mediterranean basin subsidize energy and water. The Report states that the Turkish government holds down the price of lignite, a highly polluting fuel, but that lignite use ought to be discouraged by taxing it so that users would be required to internalize the social cost of the pollution they create. This would encourage the development and use of cleaner fuels. Moreover, subsidizing energy encourages the development of heavy industries that are inappropriate for the country's resources and therefore are unlikely to be cost-effective. Each of the southern countries is faced with water shortages in the decades to come. Subsidizing water directs investment into water-intensive agricultural crops and, in addition, discourages methods for conserving water use.

Coastal cities and industries compete with tourism that requires broad clean beaches. In the light of the growing importance of tourism for earning foreign exchange, land use planning is essential. Plants and office buildings should be away from areas that compete with tourism. Economic activities in other coastal areas should be those that produce relatively little pollution, such as horticulture and certain types of service industries. Investments for air and water pollution abatement should be given a high priority, but such investments will not take place without strong incentives that require polluters to internalize their pollution. Investments in coastal wetlands should also be discouraged since wetlands help to purify the water and provide nutrition and habitat for aquatic life, which is attractive to tourists. These examples show how environmental objectives can be integrated with development objectives, which is the quintessence of sustainable development.

NOTES

1 Information for this case study was derived from Younger and Bonkoungou (1989).
2 Information for this case study was derived from Robson (1991).
3 Information for this case study was derived from Emory (1989, pp. 55–7) and Reid *et al.* (1988, 15–16).
4 Information for this case study was derived from Houseal (1990).
5 Information for this case study was derived from Reid *et al.* (1988).
6 Information for this case study was derived from Bonner (1991).
7 Information for this case study was derived from Hart (1989).
8 Information for this case study was taken from Wind and Sumardja (1988).
9 Information for this case study was derived from Hanley (1991).
10 Information for this case study was derived from Shapiro and Wainaina (1989).
11 Information for this case study was derived from the World Bank and EIB (1990).

REFERENCES

Bonner, Andrew (1991) Twilight of a tradition: Pakistan's new silk industry could put an end to the old caravan trade. *World Development*, 4(5), 15–17.

Emory, Jerry (1989) Where the sky was born. *Wilderness*, December.

Hanley, Mary L. (1991) Wave of the future? *World Development*, 4(1), 16–18.

Hart, Cherie (1989) Turning floodplains into farmland. *World Development*, 3(1), 26–8.

Houseal, Brian (1990) Maya riches. *Nature Conservancy Magazine*, May/June.

Reid, Walter V., Barnes, James N. and Blackwelder, Brent (1988) *Bankrolling Successes: A Portfolio of Sustainable Development Projects*. Washington, DC: Environmental Policy Institute and National Wildlife Federation.

Robson, Emma (1991) Sahelian Africa awaits its 'green revolution'. *World Development*, 4(6), 21–3.

Shapiro, M.W. and Wainaina, S. (1989) Kenya: a case study of the production and export of horticultural commodities. In *Successful Development in Africa*. Washington, DC: World Bank, Economic Development Institute.

Wind, Jan and Sumardja, Effendy A. (1988) World Bank irrigation and water-catchment protection project, Dumoga, Indonesia. In C. Conroy and M. Litvinoff (eds), *The Greening of Aid*. London: Earthscan Publications.

World Bank and EIB (1990) *Environmental Programme for the Mediterranean*. Washington, DC and Luxembourg: World Bank and European Investment Bank.

World Bank (1991) *World Development Report 1991*. Washington, DC: World Bank.

Younger, Steven D. and Bonkoungou, Edourd (1989) Burkina-Faso: the project Agro-Forestier. In *Successful Development in Africa: Case Studies of Projects, Programs, and Policies*. Washington, DC: World Bank.

8

Conclusions

A major conclusion of this book is that sustainable development is unlikely to replace, or become a widely recognized rival of, conventional economic development. Rather, it is altering conventional development, mainly by introducing the social costs of adverse environmental impacts and natural resource impairment into the measurement of development progress, into development strategy, and into project evaluation. Although many of the elements of sustainability will be adopted, ethical concern for the welfare of generations well into the future will probably not become a part of economic development doctrine. It will be recalled that environmental economists are not in agreement on the degree to which the welfare of future generations should be reflected in the social objective function of the present generation. There will, however, be increased concern for preserving the natural resource base.

The process of transforming conventional development economics is apparent in a number of ways. Externalities are being included in social costs to a greater degree than before, and this tendency is evident in the policies of the World Bank and other development assistance agencies. This is accompanied by a greater effort to monetize adverse environmental impacts. Although resource accounting is unlikely to be substituted for conventional national product accounts, recognition is being given to certain types of resource degradation as a social cost that should be internalized. A good example is the wide acceptance of the idea of a tax on carbon dioxide emissions as a means of reducing greenhouse gases. The use of fees or taxes on certain types of pollution and of marketable emission permits to internalize environmental costs has become popular among economists generally. The acceptance of special taxes on the consumption of polluting commodities, such as gasoline, is another example. Another way in which conventional development has moved closer to sustainable development is by the broadening of its concept of progress to include the elimination of poverty, the expansion of health and education, and the opening of economic opportunities for the rural masses in poor countries.

An important characteristic of sustainable development is its emphasis on *social* benefits and *social* costs, including nonmarket benefits and costs. Conventional development economists have identified and introduced into their analysis some of the nonmarket social costs and benefits emphasized by sustainable development economics. Since the data necessary to monetize most of these nonmarket costs and benefits are not available, they are not used in quantitative evaluations of projects.

Many of the social benefits and costs identified by sustainable development economists are not rigorously analyzed by them. Moreover, there is often a reluctance to admit that the economic benefits of certain activities may exceed the nonmarket social costs. Hence, economic activities that generate significant environmental costs that cannot be mitigated tend to be rejected. Unwillingness to consider tradeoffs between increasing the output of goods and services and incurring environmental and natural resource costs is a characteristic of the environmental movement, which is dominated by noneconomists, but environmental economists frequently follow the same path. This is often a consequence of the association of environmental economists with the environmental movement. They do not want to appear disloyal!

Conventional economic development is dominated by macroeconomic analysis: sources of economic growth; the structure of production; the role of trade, foreign investment, technological progress, and capital accumulation in growth; and the influence of fiscal, monetary, foreign exchange, and commercial policies on economic activity. By contrast, existing treatises on sustainable development are dominated by microeconomic policies almost entirely devoted to environmental and natural resource objectives. Some attention is given to income distribution and population growth in relation to development, but the analysis tends to be historical and anecdotal. Except for agriculture, little attempt is made to explore the fundamental determinants of productivity. A comprehensive treatise on sustainable development should integrate the macroeconomics of conventional development with the special concerns of natural resource sustainability and environmental protection. But unless sustainable development economists have new insights into the macroeconomics of development, such a treatise is likely to be little more than the incorporation of environmental economics into the general body of conventional economic development theory and policy. It is for this reason that I believe that sustainable development economics will not replace conventional development economics. But it is having an enormous influence on the content of conventional development.

Natural Resource Economics

In addition to making conventional economists more aware of the externalities created by man-made pollution of air, water, and soil, the major contributions by sustainable development economists have been in natural resource economics. The basic theories of exhaustible and renewable resources were formulated by conventional economists; moreover, social scientists and politicians have been worrying about running out of natural resources since Malthus. Earlier doomsday prophets who predicted the termination of world economic growth caused by natural resource exhaustion have been discredited by technological progress. The exhaustion of supplies of critical inputs, such as copper, zinc, and other metals, has been delayed, perhaps indefinitely, and technology may well provide us with an almost unlimited supply of energy. Sustainable development economists focus on the limited capacity of the environment to absorb wastes created by economic activity. There are limits to the ability of the ecosystem to assimilate municipal solid waste, toxic materials that are byproducts of industrial and agricultural production, and gases that foul our cities and collect in the upper atmosphere, without impairing the capacity of the land, water, and atmosphere to sustain life and economic activity. Therefore, an important function of the economic system should be to reduce these wastes and to change their character so that assimilation limits are not exceeded. Environmental economists are critical of conventional economics for not including waste generation and absorption in the world production function. However, sustainable development economists sometimes make apocalyptic forecasts of the destruction of the earth's capacity to sustain life as a result of waste accumulation – forecasts not supported by scientific evidence and rigorous analysis.

Robert Goodland (1991, p. 5) argues that the 'limits to growth have already been reached, that further input growth will take the planet further away from sustainability, and that we are rapidly foreclosing options for the future, possibly overshooting limits.' Evidence of these limits include: (a) human appropriation of 40 percent of the net primary product of terrestrial photosynthesis; (b) accelerating accumulation of greenhouse gases; (c) progressive destruction of the ozone shield; (d) land degradation and loss of topsoil; and (e) a high rate of loss of biodiversity (Goodland, 1991, pp. 6–12). Goodland supports his case in part by pointing to the consequences of a continuation of the current rate of Third World population growth, which will nearly double world population by 2020. However, nearly everyone would agree that per capita income growth could not be sustained over the centuries at the current rate of population growth, and that Malthusian forces will inevitably limit population growth in countries where high rates exist.

There are two weaknesses in Goodland's argument that the limit to further growth has been reached. First, there are uncertainties regarding the effects of the limits he cites on continual increases in per capita output. If population ceases to grow by late in the next century, the world may not need all the terrestrial photosynthesis for supplying food and fiber. We do not know how further accumulation of greenhouse gases will affect total agricultural productivity, given the fact that it will have favorable as well as adverse impacts on various regions in the world. The world might be able to survive ozone depletion under infrared screening shields. We can only speculate on the economic effects of biodiversity. A second weakness, which I regard as more important, is the implicit assumption that technology and a change in world production and consumption practices cannot reduce waste generation to keep it within the absorptive capacity of the environment, while permitting an indefinite increase in per capita income. Will today's pessimistic forecasts of economic growth again be negated by accelerated technological progress?

A different question is whether the world will devote sufficient labor, capital, and technology to reduce waste generation (by recycling, energy substitution, and increased efficiency). If not, the real limitation is political will.

Sustainable development economists regard natural resources as natural capital, which is more limited in supply than man-made capital. They argue that the depletion and degradation of natural capital in the course of economic activity should be treated as a social cost analogous to the depreciation of bridges and machinery. Private financial accounting recognizes the depreciation of certain types of natural resources, and tax systems provide depreciation allowances for mineral reserves. Natural resource capital depreciation should be treated as a social cost in shaping economic policies and, for certain purposes, in national accounting. This practice should be adopted by conventional economic development.

Some sustainable development economists have emphasized limitations on the substitution of man-made capital for natural capital and suggest that in allocating natural resources among different uses we should choose the use that maximizes the net present social value of the resource. This approach assumes that supplies of capital and labor are infinitely elastic, while the resource in question is a unique entity. Given these assumptions, this approach is in line with conventional economics. However, in a macroeconomic context in which the prices of capital, labor, and resource rents are not given, this approach cannot determine the allocation of all productive resources that will maximize the present value of the net social product.

Moreover, it is possible to increase the supply of renewable natural resources and even the effective supply of exhaustible resources through the application of new technology and capital.

Herman E. Daly (1991, p. 18) advances the thesis that 'economic policy should be designed to increase the productivity of natural capital and its total amount, rather than to increase the productivity of man-made capital and its accumulation, as was appropriate in the past when it was the limiting factor.' Daly supports his argument by stating that the possibility of substitution of capital for natural resources is very limited, but that since man-made capital requires natural resources, there is more complementarity than substitutability between the two. 'The neoclassical assumption of near perfect substitutability between natural resources and man-made capital is a serious distortion of reality' (Daly, 1991, p. 20). Although Daly is right in emphasizing the limited supply of natural resources, we should not downgrade capital accumulation. The fact that capital and technology developed by capital investment can be used to increase the supply and efficiency of natural resources means that economic policy should be directed both to capital accumulation and its productivity, and to the supply and productivity of natural resources. Capital accumulation requires savings, which means reducing consumption, but the savings can be used to produce capital goods for producing more consumer goods and services, or they can be directed to increasing the supply and productivity of natural resources. In this sense, there is complementarity between increases in the supply of capital and natural resources, and not just complementarity in the sense that producing capital goods requires more natural resources.

Perhaps Daly's analysis is indicative of the general neglect of saving and capital accumulation by sustainable development economists. The industrial countries, and especially the USA, will require a substantial rise in savings rates if they are to devote sufficient resources to keep waste generation within the absorptive capacity of the environment, and to reverse the global trend of natural resource depletion and degradation. A shortage of capital may be a major constraint on sustainable development.

Divorcing Economics from Ideology

Sustainable development economics needs to be separated from the ideology and ethical doctrines of the conservation and ecological movements if it is to broaden its audience. Sustainable development economists also need to specify an aggregative objective function that will encompass its principles. Maximizing net social benefits within the constraint of Pareto optimality constitutes an aggregative objective that could be formulated to include the sustainability criteria. This can be done by rigorously defining sustainability and by treating measurable departures from sustainability as social costs in the objective function. As long as sustainable development economists persist in using vague ideological concepts of sustainability, it cannot be integrated with an economic theory of development. Talking vaguely about preserving the ability of future generations to increase their per capita incomes is more philosophy than economics. As is suggested in Chapter 2, preserving the productivity of the natural resource base and treating reductions in that productivity as a social cost are a potentially workable approach.

Reform of Foreign Aid

The environmentalists' case against most foreign aid goes well beyond the charge of supporting environmentally flawed projects. They have challenged the traditional view that favors natural resource exploitation for increasing export earnings and industrialization as primary contributors to economic growth. Moreover, they believe that much of the external loan assistance is contravening sustainable development by destroying the natural resource base, perpetuating low productivity of the masses, and burdening the economies with debt that has largely gone to finance upper-class consumption and projects that mainly benefit an affluent minority. Although such adverse criticisms are not wholly warranted, the positive recommendations made by environmentalists for increasing the proportion of foreign assistance going to agriculture and small enterprise development, education and social services, and environmental protection and resource conservation are gaining wide support among students of economic development. Despite the large inflow of capital to Third World countries during the 1970s and 1980s, nearly one-third of the population in all developing countries live below the poverty line, and 70 percent of the population of the least developed do so (UNDP, 1991, p. 153). Per capita consumption declined over the past decade in Latin America and sub-Saharan Africa, and an estimated one-fifth of the population of all developing countries go hungry every day. The estimate of one billion people living in absolute poverty remains the same in 1991 as it was 30 years ago, and the current estimate is probably an understatement. The growth of total factor productivity in Third World countries declined from an annual rate of 1.3 percent in 1960–73 to a negative rate of 0.2 percent in 1974–87, with an even larger decline for Latin America and Africa (World Bank, 1991, p. 43). As the *World Development Report 1991* points out, the 'association between productivity growth and aggregate growth is strong and positive . . . and it holds across regions and in differing periods' (p. 45). The Report also states that economic policies explain much of the difference in productivity growth. This record underlies the view of environmental economists that foreign aid has not been making a significant contribution to sustainable development.

The positive recommendations of environmental economists for increasing the proportion of foreign assistance going to agriculture and small enterprise development, education, health and other social services, and environmental protection and resource conservation are gaining wide support among many students of economic development, including some of the economists working in multilateral development banks (MDBs). This appears to be having an influence on the policies and loan portfolios of the MDBs.

Encouraging Governments to Promote Sustainable Development

MDBs, the UN agencies, the OECD, and the conservation NGOs have played an important role in popularizing the principles of sustainable development, and environmental economists have formulated methods of implementing these principles in development policies and programs. It is somewhat ironic that the MDBs, which have been the object of severe criticism by conservation groups for violating environmental and natural resource management principles, are now the leading proponents of sustainable development in Third World countries. The most important job of the MDBs and other multilateral and bilateral assistance agencies is to convert Third World and Eastern European governments to sustainable development. This will not be easy to do. Many Third World leaders are suspicious of the environmental movement in the developed countries and fear it will work against their interests. First, it is feared that import restrictions, imposed either because products do not meet health and sanitation standards in the importing country, or because the method of production does not meet developed-country environmental production standards, will harm the markets for Third World goods. Second, there is a concern that environmental conditions attached to foreign aid will impinge on the sovereignty of states to control their internal economies. Third, there is the concern that governments of developing countries may be pressured to take measures in the interest of the global environment, for which they are not properly compensated by developed countries. Finally, the governments of poor developing countries are under political pressure to provide short-term improvements in per capita income at the expense of measures promoting sustainability. Sustainable development is a revolutionary political and social concept. It will not succeed without the conviction and participation of the masses of people who must bring it about. Gaining that conviction and participation is a more important challenge for external assistance agencies than providing capital and technical assistance.

REFERENCES

Daly, Herman (1991) From empty-world economics to full-world economics: recognizing an historical turning point in economic development. In R. Goodland *et al.* (eds), *Environmentally Sustainable Economic Development: Building on Brundtland*, Environmental Working Paper no. 46. Washington, DC: World Bank.

Goodland, Robert (1991) The case that the world has reached limits. In R. Goodland *et al.* (eds), *Environmentally Sustainable Economic Development: Building on Brundtland*, Environmental Working Paper no. 46. Washington, DC: World Bank.

UNDP (1991) *Human Development Report 1991*. New York: Oxford University Press for the United Nations Development Program.

World Bank (1991) *World Development Report 1991*. Washington, DC: World Bank.

Index